Speaking in Stories

Resources for Christian Storytellers

WILLIAM R. WHITE

AUGSBURG Publishing House • Minneapolis

SPEAKING IN STORIES

Copyright © 1982 Augsburg Publishing House

Library of Congress Catalog Card No. 82-70954

International Standard Book No. 0-8066-1929-5

Scripture quotations unless otherwise noted are from the Revised Standard Version of the Bible, copyright 1946, 1952, and 1971 by the Division of Christian Education of the National Council of Churches.

Scripture quotations marked TEV are from the Good News Bible, Today's English Version: copyright © American Bible Society 1966, 1971, 1976. Used by permission.

The story "Silence" beginning on page 114 is excerpted from *The Town Beyond the Wall* by Elie Wiesel. Translated by Stephen Becker. Copyright © 1964 by Elie Wiesel. Reprinted by permission of Holt, Rinehart and Winston, Publishers.

MANUFACTURED IN THE UNITED STATES OF AMERICA

98 97   9   10   11   12   13   14   15   16   17

To Sara and Scott,
my favorite story listeners

Contents

A Personal Journey

At one time a person's wealth was judged more by stories told than by material possessions. By these standards I had an uncle who was an extremely wealthy man.

Douglas, or Stub as he was known to his neighbors, was a great teller of tales. When he spun his story, he would assume the character of the person involved. He had mastered the voices and mannerisms of dozens of the most colorful people from his small, rural Wisconsin community—the drawl of Albert Warn, the high-pitched tone of Billy Hindeberger.

In the summers of my youth I would visit his farm to drive tractor during haying season. At night the men would gather at the barbershop to pass time and information during those pretelevision days. "I finished haying the back forty and have moved to that piece 'cross from the barn." "I heard Vernon hit Bob Ross's dog with the milk truck yesterday morning." "How'd you like loadin' round bales?"

As they sat together, they laughed, told of sickness, planned the next work crew, and kept in touch with each other as well as those who were absent. The Rural Electrification Administration was only now reaching some of their small Wisconsin farms, and time was still slow. They still shared work; they still spent time together.

Although I enjoyed the farm talk, I was impatient for the stories to begin. If someone would just tell one, I knew a whole flood of them would follow. The most natural response to one story is another story.

In that small barbershop, the other men would tell their stories as a kind of prelude to the main event. Then, when he felt ready, my uncle would begin to tell his story. His voice would whine or crack or stutter, depending on the characters in the story. First an imaginary telephone might be at his ear as he told one of the countless tales that arose from the days of the party line. Then he might start a make-believe motor to get us into the next tale.

Most often the stories were true, with necessary embellishments added for the sake of the art. Nearly all of the stories were humorous, but they were told in a way that only added dignity to the persons involved, not to ridicule them. Though it is now 25 years later, I still remember the punch lines: "Beauty is only skin deep, but ugliness goes clear to the bone." "I've got a dog from every town, but they're all rat terriers." More important, because I learned to know them through the eyes of my uncle, I remember and respect the people that still live in that small farming community.

That was my introduction to the art of the storyteller. It was a delightful and enchanting experience. I soon began to test my own prowess by telling stories to my younger brother, Norm, in our shared bedroom. On Saturday mornings I would tell him tales of a group of 11 boys called the League of Nations Gang. The stories were exploits of Swedish twins, an American Indian, a black youth, and a smattering of white folks, all who were adopted by the same family.

My brother would listen intently as I told of their adventures. At times danger would strike, and one of the boys would be killed. Norm would cry, "Don't let him die, Bill, don't let him die." Through the magic of the storyteller, the dead youth would be brought back to life again, and the story would continue. In my bedroom I learned of the power possessed by a teller of stories.

It was many years before I even began to think of storytelling as something that could be used in the church. Then, in the summer of 1960, I packed my hiking boots and idealism and headed from rural Wisconsin to a camp in upstate New York populated by young blacks, whites, and Puerto Ricans from Manhattan's lower east side. Although my experience with anyone whose ancestry did not originate in Scandinavia was negligible (it was said of my small town that even the dogs barked in Norwegian), I was convinced that there was no obstacle too difficult, no challenge too great for those who had faith.

It took but a few hours for the cultural shock to set in. Initially I didn't even understand the language. "Bad" meant good, "boss action" meant super. My tennis shoes were "sneakers" and the pop I drank was "soda." If they weren't correcting me, they were bringing their friends in to listen to me talk.

Perhaps the most perplexing adjustment for me was in trying to relate my biblical faith to 13-to-15-year-old boys who had seldom entered the door of a church. The evening devotions I had planned were meaningless. I soon discovered the only link: the boys were moviegoers who seldom missed any film that came to their neighborhood theater. Our evening discussions quickly became story hours, beginning with "The

Ten Commandments" or "David and Bathsheba" as the text, slowly moving through the actual Bible story, and then into the stories of our own lives.

Several years and a divinity degree later, I discovered the joy of the story in my rural congregations in southern Wisconsin. In those rigid, serious church services, the story was an occasion of relief and delight. As I began one of my tales, arms would uncross, brows would unfurrow, and people would lean forward. While they seemed to tolerate the sermons, they celebrated the stories.

From rural Wisconsin I was called as director of a group of church camps in Michigan. For nine years my classrooms were around campfires and under oak trees. In this unsophisticated atmosphere, where neither chalkboards nor film projectors are to be found, a teacher must learn to rely on a portable curriculum. Under these conditions, the story is king.

At present I am engaged in a search, along with thousands of other Christian teachers and pastors, for a meaningful way to proclaim the message of Jesus for our day. The method I seek, like the message itself, must be simple, direct, and concrete. It must be filled with pictures in order that the imaginations of people can be opened to the ever-new and joyous message of the gospel. It is my conviction that, as we return to a renewed interest in the message of Jesus, we also must take a new look at his method of communicating that message. It is again time for the church to learn to speak in stories.

1

The Appeal of Storytelling

When someone says "Let me tell you a story" or "Once upon a time," we immediately sense a bit of excitement, a bit of magic in the air. If it is a formal occasion, we see people relax, and we can feel a sense of anticipation. The story can, as J. R. R. Tolkien has said, ". . . give to the child or man that hears it . . . a catch of the breath, a beat and lifting of the heart. . . ." This is true, but why? How can we explain this response?

Stories Are Gospel Language

Though nearly all of Scripture, from Genesis to Revelation, moves by narrative and story, it is Jesus who is the perfecter of the form. Through vivid pictures of seeds, pearls, and unemployed workers, he helps us imagine the kingdom of God. Through parables of lost children and dishonest servants, he invites us to picture a gracious and loving parent. Virtually nothing Jesus says is found in lecture form; instead, every word the gospels record is communicated through metaphor, parable, or simile.

In the story, then, we come closer to gospel language than in any other literary or oral communication form. It is in the story that we know of God's entry into our world and our redemption. Christians find the story appealing because it is the language of revelation, the language of God's love, the language of Jesus. It may even be true, as Elie Wiesel has said, that "God made man because he loves stories."

Stories Are a Living Language

Alas, much of the speech that we hear is lifeless and dull, making the story, by contrast, a most pleasant exception. In the church we listen to lectures that are primarily abstract in nature. Sermons are full of ideas, classrooms deal with concepts, and church leaders, lay and clergy alike, seem to be enamored with doctrine and the kind of thought that seems a far journey from where we live.

Sallie TeSelle has written that where ". . . theology becomes overly abstract, conceptual and systematic, it separates thought and life, belief and practice, words and their embodiment, making it more difficult, if not impossible for us to believe in our hearts what we confess with our lips."

There is a distance between the listener and abstract language that does not exist in the world of story. Our lives are stories and, in a sense, any good story is about us. We are drawn to the story because with little effort we can place ourselves in the midst of the drama.

Unlike abstract thinking, story is living language. It is real. It is concrete. It is made from the same fabric that shapes our lives. Though we struggle over the meaning of an abstract thought, we understand the story.

As a type of picture language, stories help us see, help us

understand, even when we don't want to see. It was through parable that Jesus exposed the misconceptions of his enemies. It was through story and metaphor that the prophets, Israel's ophthalmologists, corrected the astigmatism of God's people, helping them to see the connection between faith and justice. Nathan, one of these doctors, was King David's personal physician.

When Bathsheba, wife of the soldier Uriah, became pregnant by David, the king arranged for Uriah to return from battle and visit his wife. Refusing to enjoy the comforts of home while his comrades were still in the ravages of war, Uriah declined to sleep with his wife. In desperation, David returned Uriah to the front and arranged his death. After the period of mourning, David married the widow Bathsheba.

Shortly after the birth of the baby, Nathan arrived unexpectedly at the palace. (This was one doctor who made house calls.) "Let me tell you a story," he began. "There were two men who lived in the same city, one rich, the other poor. The rich man had many sheep, the poor man had a single ewe lamb which he and his children raised as a household pet. When visitors came to the home of the rich man, instead of slaughtering one of his own flock, he took the lamb of the poor man and served it to his visitors."

David was incensed. "As the Lord lives, the man who has done this deserves to die."

Nathan shot out his finger at David and said, "You are that man!"

Although a great and honest man and a good king, David learned that day of the enormous power of self-deception. He had convinced himself that the king was slightly above the law. Nathan stripped him of his illusion and helped him to see. He did it with a story.

Stories Give Joy

Perhaps the greatest and most obvious appeal of storytelling is that it is a particularly joyful experience. Nearly any story, well told, is fun for the listener. Is it because stories frequently leave people living "happily ever after"? Is it, as J. R. R. Tolkien has written, that story, and particularly the fairy story, denies universal final defeat, giving us a glimpse of ultimate joy? Is it because the good story allows us to use our childlike powers of fantasy and escape the world we live in? Is it because stories deal with mystery and awe in an age where practical people rid the world of a reason to wonder? In a story-shaped world it is not so. The princess is returned to life by love's first kiss, the workers hired at the end of the day receive the same reward as those who bore the burden of the day, and the tiny tailor, through no great skill of his own, becomes king. There is a strange and wonderful grace at work in the story world, and it is enough to give even the most hardened cynic reason to hope.

Perhaps it is for all these reasons that we look forward to the storyteller's art. When we hear the story, we understand it; it is joyous, it gives us a sense of hope. In a world dark with fear, that may be reason enough to begin to speak in stories.

2

Learning to Tell Stories

There was once a rabbi whose grandfather had been a disciple of the Baal Shem and who was asked to tell a story about him. He said:

My grandfather was lame. Once they asked him to tell a story about his teacher. And he related how the holy Baal Shem used to hop and dance while he prayed. My grandfather rose as he spoke, and he was so swept away by his story that he himself began to hop and dance to show how the master had done. From that hour on he was cured of his lameness. That's the way to tell a story!

Martin Buber
Tales of the Hasidim: The Early Masters

What a treat it is to hear a story told by someone totally immersed in the tale. Every gesture, every facial expression, every tone of voice seems only to add to the impact of the story. But if that is what it takes to tell a story, then there will be very few of us who even dare begin. If all of us must be Lawrence Oliviers before we can act, there will be precious little theater.

What we know, of course, is that there are as many different styles of telling stories as there are people or stories. Some people use every muscle in their bodies, others barely move during the telling of the tale, letting their voices and eyes make the impact.

What we also know is that most of you reading this book are already storytellers. It is a rare day when you don't share the events of your lives with someone else. You tell your friends, and anyone else who will listen, of the amazing exploits of your three-year-old child. You recount a particularly exciting personal adventure. How often have you told the story about the time you locked yourself out of the house? Our lives are stories, and as we share the events of our lives we engage in storytelling.

That does not mean that all storytellers or the stories they tell are entertaining. Many are downright boring. But just as most of us need a bit of instruction in order to play an instrument or learn a craft, some reflection on the art of the storyteller can help us to tell our stories in a more attractive and entertaining manner.

An Intimate Art

The beauty of the simple art of storytelling is its intimacy. As the story unfolds, each listener feels as if he or she alone is being addressed; storytelling, regardless of the size of the group, is always one-to-one. Put a lectern between the storyteller and the listeners, and a bit of that intimacy is lost. Add even such a small object as a book, and the closeness is further eroded.

The ancients were well aware of the sense of community

that develops around the story. American Indians gathered cross-legged in a circle when stories were told. The storyteller sat in the same position, but within the circle.

Like the Indians, most storytellers understand their place within the community: they are not so much doing something *for* a group as *with* it. The method they use is significant. Most storytellers prefer to seek the same level as the listeners. If the listeners sit, the storyteller sits. One stands only if it is necessary to be seen. Unlike the lecturer, the storyteller is naturally a part of the group.

Intimacy is the primary reason that the story is told rather than read. Just as a suitor would not read a proposal to his beloved, just as a mother would not read tender advice to her daughter from a prepared text, so the storyteller chooses to tell the story from the heart rather than read it from the page. Granted, more preparation time is needed when the story is told, but, as in the making of homemade bread, the extra effort is well worthwhile.

How to Begin Telling Stories

1. Read stories—lots of stories. In your reading, note how some authors write for the ear (these are the stories you want) while others write for the eye. Many modern stories are primarily literary in nature—the emphasis is more on style than on plot—while those of such authors as Elie Wiesel and Leo Tolstoy are written the way we speak. Nearly all biblical stories have an "oral voice" that allows them to be told easily. Consider the story of Jonah or the New Testament parable of the good Samaritan. Most biblical stories hold images that remain strong and clear to the modern listener. 2. From your reading, select a simple story. For this first

venture, the story should take no longer than three or four minutes to tell. Read the story 10 or 15 times, until you have a firm grasp of it.

3. Prepare by reading aloud. Though you may feel foolish talking to the walls, there really is no other way to discover how the story sounds or which words you should select. An oral event needs oral preparation.

4. Normally it is best to memorize your story incident by incident rather than word for word to avoid making the story sound stiff and wooden. After reading most stories 15 times, you may find you need not memorize. The exceptions to this rule include the literal method of telling Bible stories (see Chapter 4) and essential phrases that need precise language.

5. Cut the excess words. Most stories, whether they are told formally or informally, fail because we say too much. The model story can be found in the parables of Jesus where there are virtually no wasted words. The rule is: If it is not necessary to the story, eliminate it.

6. Find an audience and begin. I have been blessed with two children who love stories and normally form a willing audience. If you don't have children, borrow some.

7. Use your living-room voice. Avoid both the preacher's stained-glass voice or the affected voice of the actor. I find that seating people intimately in a circle or moving closer to those who form the audience helps keep my voice natural. Though some people with high voices may need to use the lower register of their speaking voices, most people should be able to speak as if they are talking with friends.

8. You may wish to make use of a tape recorder to record your first few stories. This unbiased critic can help you avoid those little verbal mannerisms, the "uhs" and the "ums," that sneak into the storyteller's oral art.

What to Avoid in Storytelling

Like most tasks, common sense and intuition will carry the beginning storyteller much more faithfully than a set of rules. Perhaps I have already exceeded the limit, but just in case you are still a bit faint of heart, here are a few additional guidelines, put in the negative form.

1. Don't rush. Tempo is as important to a good story as it is to a fine song. The tendency to rush is particularly great in the beginner, for fear seems to speed us up, as if to say, "Let's get this thing over quickly." Allow pauses to fit naturally into your story. Like the layout of a good advertisement, the spaces between the words are often as important as the words themselves. Pauses allow excitement to build and invite the listeners' imaginations to soar.

2. Avoid distractive visual aids. Rather than help a story, most objects used in storytelling hinder the natural communication between the storyteller and the audience. One of the most popular props, the flannelgraph, is particularly difficult to use effectively. As the storyteller turns to place objects on the board, visual contact is lost. I have used a flannel vest on occasion to tell stories in order not to lose eye contact. I simply place the objects on my vest while facing the audience. Though the vest adds a nice touch, I feel even it can get in the way of the contact between storyteller and audience.

If you use a picture, let it be rather abstract, allowing the imagination full range. Though I am reluctant even to use pictures, I have had to show a portrait of Martin Luther on Reformation Sunday. I discovered that children assumed I was talking about the great civil rights leader. Now I show the picture briefly before I begin, then I place it face down as I tell the story.

3. Avoid lecturing or attaching morals to your stories. Noth-

ing ruins a story faster than following it up with an explanation. If you respect your listeners enough to tell the story, respect them enough to let them draw their own conclusions. "He who has ears to hear, let him hear."

If a discussion develops following the story, the storyteller is allowed, in my opinion, to enter the discussion, but with no more authority over the interpretation than anyone else. Unlike a speaker's lecture, the story has an independent existence.

4. Don't confuse stories with illustrations. Illustrations are incomplete; they point to a greater meaning. The story has its own meaning. With rare exception did Jesus "explain" his parables, and then only upon request at a later time.

3

Where Can I Use Stories?

How we say something can be as important as what we say, or, as in the case of the gospel, can be identified with what we say. For Jesus, method and message are one. His gospel can no more be conveyed with abstract language than can good wine be stored in paper cartons. Love is an action, not an idea. Forgiveness is an event, not a concept. The gospel Jesus proclaimed was not a new teaching, nor even a new experience; it was a history, a story. Story is the speech form of the gospel.

Few of us can imagine children sitting in rows as Jesus paces back and forth lecturing on the difference between consubstantiation and transubstantiation. His message demanded that the method he use be descriptive, concrete, and full of pictures. To announce the kingdom of God, he used parables, metaphors, and similes. Jesus was a storytelling man.

If we are to be faithful to the carpenter's message, we also will need to be faithful to his method. Preachers, teachers, and other leaders need to see that if they use a different method, they may get a different message. Like their Lord, Christian communicators should also be storytellers.

Stories in Education

Many centuries ago, a rich caliph in Baghdad gave a banquet in honor of the birth of his son. All the nobility who partook of the feast brought costly gifts, each one except a young sage named Mehelled Abi, who came empty-handed. He explained to the caliph: "Today the young prince will receive many precious gifts, jewels and rare coins. My gift is different. From the time he is old enough to listen until manhood, I will come to the palace and tell him stories of our Arabian heroes. When he becomes our ruler, he will be just and honest."

The young sage kept his word. When the prince was at last made caliph, he became famous for his wisdom and honor. To this day, an inscription on a scroll in Budapest reads "It was because of the seed sown by the tales."

In my youth I grew up on a steady diet of biblical stories taught by Gertrud, Norris, and Ted Borgen. They were the Mehelled Abis of my life. If faith has indeed taken root in me, if good has been done, my scroll too should read: "It was because of the seed sown by the tales."

We can be appointed to no more noble or important task in our churches than to share the stories of God with children. As in the case of the young prince, what is imprinted deeply on our minds in our youth shapes who we are and what we shall become. The stories, the dreams we live by, are vital in our growth as children of God.

In fact, unless we learn to know the stories and events, the dreams and aspirations, the promises and pledges that shaped our biblical ancestors, how shall we grow into our baptism as members of the family of God? It is through reading and, more importantly, the faithful witness of others that we become aware of our family history.

In Chapter 2 are some guidelines to help people begin to tell stories. That, of course, is not the end of it. After "How do I tell stories?" the most frequently asked question is "What should I do *after* I tell the story?" There is a variety of good responses to that question. The first is: *Do nothing!* Let the story sink in. Don't be afraid of silence.

At times the story will elicit questions. I am quick to answer the questions that ask "What did you say?" and slow to answer the ones that ask "What does that mean?" Although I love to discuss the story, I resist interpreting it. The more quickly I explain everything, the sooner the discussion ends. It is easier for students not to think when the teacher gives all the answers.

Occasionally, after the completion of the story, I invite the listeners to retell the narrative through the eyes of one of the characters in the story. For example, after telling the story "The Prodigal Son," I might say, "I would like you to sit in groups of three or four and each retell the story from the point of view of one of the persons in the story. Please use first person. If you choose to tell the story like the older brother, you might begin, 'I want to tell you the story of my good-for-nothing younger brother.'" The insights into the parable as a result of using this approach frequently are amazing. The discussion that follows can be lively.

Still another response is to ask the group a single question after the story is told. I once asked a confirmation class, upon completion of the story "Joseph and the Coat of Many Colors," if any of them thought their parents ever played favorites. The discussion lasted until the end of the hour, with frequent references to the original story. Stories can be a stepping-stone to significant class involvement if the storyteller can refrain from imposing his or her own interpretation on the listeners.

Teaching is not a simple task, but we frequently make it more difficult than it has to be. Teachers expend great energy finding or making things that will be "interesting" or developing nice little "projects" that are only marginally related to the lesson in order to keep the children interested. We dare not forget that our primary task is to leave our students with the stories of God. There is no more direct or effective way to do this than to tell the story.

Stories in Preaching

There is nothing in the church that can benefit more from a good dose of storytelling than the sermon. Carefully schooled in the abstract method of "doing theology," my generation spent long hours in dusty libraries reading articles like: "A Method for Identifying Redactional Passages in Matthew on Functional and Linguistic Grounds." No wonder our sermons often sound like term papers.

In all of our preparation for preaching, little thought was given to the unique oral nature of the gospel. Armed with a full-length manuscript and aided by excellent scholarship, our sermons provided parishioners with plenty of information about Christianity. However, information is not what people lack. The goal of preaching is not to inform; what preaching is about is inviting people to faith. Through the spoken word, we are to help people make connections between the biblical word and the stories of their lives. Like our Lord, we are to assist our hearers in envisioning something as radically new and different as the kingdom of God.

How long have we lived with the complaints of ministers that the actions of Christians seem to be uninformed by their theological beliefs? Pulpit talk has regularly decried the tendency to divorce religion from life. Is it also possible to make this charge against a significant number of sermons? Perhaps a part of the inability to connect the sacred and the secular can be traced to the nature of the sermon itself. Perhaps the theology most frequently offered comes in a form not easily translated into concrete acts of discipleship. Alive and dynamic, the story helps us to see the connection between the gospel events and the events of our lives.

To preach in a manner that invites connections is always difficult, but without sharing the connections in one's own life it is nearly impossible. It is not enough for me as preacher to share only what I think. In order for theology to become alive, people need to see how the word has become flesh in me. Without pretending to be a norm, I must allow people to see where the word of forgiveness and hope and redemption has touched and shaped me. In short, I must become transparent and invite the listener to see how The Story touches my own personal story.

Story resources for the proclaimer are many. Through parable, fairy tale, modern short story, or autobiography, the preacher can suggest connections between the Word of Life and the words of our lives. Slowly we see that the story of Jesus and our stories are one. For this to happen, the preacher must become a storyteller.

In his paper "The Preacher As Storyteller," Professor Charles Rice says: "Far from trying to make of the preacher an artist who writes timeless phrases, I am interested more in learning how to live and speak in community, in the form that most human beings use in communicating meaning, celebrating, and marking off time: by storytelling."

Professor Rice says he finds many benefits in storytelling. Not only is the content of sermons changed as one uses stories, but the method is improved, delivery is energized, theological jargon diminishes, and the stained-glass voice of the preacher disappears. Sermons become less formal, more like animated conversation.

Again, a story is not the same as an illustration. An illustration is usually a canned anecdote that one finds in a magazine or an alphabetized book of sermon helps. But the more important difference is this: The illustration always needs to be explained; it points to a different reality. The story is its own reality. What we are encouraging is the use of stories that stand on their own.

At times the story is most effective when separated from the sermon. Perhaps a hymn can be sung between the story and the sermon. This gives the story room and allows the preacher to shift gears before moving from story to interpretation.

At other times the story fits well into the sermon. It is one more piece of what the preacher is attempting to proclaim. It can come directly before the sermon or it may be at the conclusion. At the end, the story leaves the conclusion up to the hearer.

Storytelling and Camping

Outside of church school, camping is the largest and most effective lay ministry in the church. Each year thousands of high school and college-age people are engaged as counselors at our summer camps. In a span of five or six days, camp counselors will spend more hours with children than church school teachers or pastors will manage in an entire year. Counselors become instant heroes, and since they share the dirt and grime of a week's existence, their credibility often soars to an amazing height.

Campers soon trust their counselors with their dreams and most cherished secrets. Questions that are never raised in the classroom, or even at home, seem to come out easily as a youngster stares into the dancing flames of a campfire or at the dark ceiling of a cabin late at night.

What a grand opportunity the job of counselor provides. What an awesome responsibility. How will the church help counselors to prepare for this ministry? Few have seminary or Bible school training. Since most staff come directly from campuses to camp, there is no time for a lengthy training period. How can the church help these dedicated people prepare to lead Bible studies and cabin devotions?

Rather than attempt to make counselors into systematic theologians in two weeks, why not help them become storytellers? During their training, surround them with Bible stories told in an engaging manner. Teach them some of the marvelous legends associated with the faith and acquaint them with the lives of the saints. Next add a few sessions on the simple methods of storytelling, and invite them to practice telling stories to each other.

While we are at it, teach a few exciting longer tales for those who seem to have a penchant for the story so that there can be some long adventures told around the campfires. Encourage the imaginative to develop legends to explain prominent features of the land around the camp. If there is time, allow someone to study the rich Indian lore of the area.

If there are musicians in the group (and which camp doesn't have at least two or three?), let them develop ballads to be sung. Below is the song that was written with the help of some counselors after I told the story of David. It is sung to the tune of "Davy Crockett" from the Walt Disney motion picture.

Ballad of King David

Chorus: David, Son of Jesse
                 King of Israel

Learned to play the harp as shepherd boy
His psalms and songs brought love and joy.
Invited to the palace to sing for the king.
A peaceful sleep to Saul he did bring. (chorus)

Goliath was challenging the men of Saul
Dressed in steel, he stood nine feet tall
David met the challenge with a prayer and a sling
With the giant's death, new hope he did bring. (chorus)

David was a hero both far and near
"Why, he's greater than the king" he heard the people cheer
Saul became angry and threatened his life
David fled the city with the help of his wife. (chorus)

For many years he roamed the land
David spared Saul's life when it was in his hand
At the end, when King Saul died
David, who still loved him, lay down and cried. (chorus)

David loved Bathsheba and, to his shame,
He killed Uriah to hide their game.
Nathan the prophet called the king to repent
With sackcloth and ashes, his clothes he rent. (chorus)

His land was biggest, his land was best
From Tadmor in the East to Joppa in the West
Poetry flourished, music was at hand
People worshiped Yahweh throughout the land. (chorus)

Though the ballad isn't great poetry, it helped our staff remember the story.

Stories are portable. They do not require paper and pencil. They can be told as effectively at the base of a tree as in a classroom. Storytelling is a marvelous companion for the church camper.

_4_

Telling Bible Stories

When the great rabbi Baal Shem-Tov felt that his people were threatened, he would go to a secret part of the forest to meditate. There he would light a special fire, say a special prayer, and the disaster would be averted.

When his successor faced similar circumstances, he would go to the same place in the forest and pray: "Great Master of the Universe, I do not know how to light the special fire, but I am able to say the special prayer, and this must be sufficient." It was, and the disaster was averted.

When his successor faced difficult times, he would go to the special place in the forest on behalf of his Jewish people and pray: "Great Master of the Universe, I do not know how to light the fire, I do not know how to say the prayer, but I know the place, and this must be sufficient." It was sufficient, and the disaster was once again averted.

When it fell to his successor to deal with the misfortune of his people, he sat in his armchair with palms uplifted. "Great Master of the Universe," he prayed, "I am unable to light the special fire, I do not know the prayer, I cannot even find the place in the forest, but I can tell the story, and this must be sufficient." And it was.

The eyewitnesses to the gospel events have long since passed on to their reward. We no longer know the secret places and the special prayers that brought biblical people into close encounters with God. All that remains is the story, but it is sufficient.

We Christians believe and confess that in the story of Israel, the story of Jesus, we find our own story. James Carroll has suggested that we can define faith in this manner. "Belief," he writes, "is what happens when the story of Jesus and my story become experienced as inseparably one."

As I hear of Jonah, I immediately am put in touch with my constant flight to avoid the mission God lays at my door. I too am unwilling to walk through foreign streets, to go to unknown places for fear God will connect me with the lives of those I neither know nor understand.

I listen to the tales of impetuous Peter who failed more often than he succeeded. I see him falling in the water, boldly predicting his eternal fidelity, irrelevantly volunteering to build a monument to Jesus when it would have been far more appropriate to remain silent, and denying his Lord at the moment of crisis. Perhaps that is why I love him so—I see so much of myself in this man of extremes. If he is a saint of God, there is hope for the likes of me.

The people of the Bible are accessible to us in a unique way. Though their faith is lauded, their darker sides are not hidden. The tales of Abraham, Moses, and David not only cheer their achievements but also expose their weaknesses and vulnerabilities. Knowing both their faithfulness and their unfaithfulness makes them more available to us. Let the storyteller, like the biblical writer, hide nothing in telling the story.

31

Methods of Telling Bible Stories

It is not difficult to find stories in the Bible. Contrary to what some would have us believe, story, not doctrine, is the Bible's main ingredient. We do not have a doctrine of creation, we have stories of creation. We do not have a concept of the resurrection, we have marvelous narratives of Easter. There is relatively little in either the Old Testament or the New Testament that does not rest on narrative or story of some form.

Furthermore, to the storyteller's delight, most biblical stories have been lifted directly from the mouths of the ancient storytellers and placed immediately on the page. Unlike many modern literary pieces that are penned primarily to be read, nearly all Bible stories were intended to be heard. It is this "oral voice" that allows the Bible story to be told powerfully 1900 years later.

Bible storytellers can use either the literal method or the adaption method for telling their stories. Most use the second method, adaption. Using contemporary language, this form of telling attempts to bridge the two centuries of time that separate the original event from today's hearing.

Adaption is necessary for many of the finer Old Testament tales that normally are too long to be told unless they are edited. The David story that follows later in this chapter is compiled from resources in 1 Chronicles, 1 and 2 Samuel, and Psalms. Even after selecting only a small portion of the available material, the story still takes nearly 20 minutes to tell.

Though the adaption of a biblical story takes less time to prepare than telling it word for word, study and preparation are indispensable for a good telling. The best adaptions stick fairly close to the text, adding information only when necessary to the telling. Thus it is important to begin preparation by selecting a good Bible translation. Though the newer translations are often easier for most people to understand, they lack a richness in language and are not nearly as memorable. "Am I supposed to take care of my brother?" in the Cain and Abel story is far less striking to me than "Am I my brother's keeper?" Words are the raw materials for the story-teller's craft and must be selected carefully, asking, "Which phrase is most likely to leave an imprint on the mind?"

After the selection of a translation, a bit of research is in order. The storyteller will not use all the information gathered, but it is essential to understand some of the customs and geography of the story that are unfamiliar to us today. In the story we normally call "The Good Samaritan," it is important that we understand the trip from Jerusalem to Jericho was a hazardous journey. The 17-mile route, winding around large rocks and dropping thousands of feet, was a robber's delight. Likewise, in the story of "The Prodigal Son," it is important to help the listener understand the significance of a Jewish boy feeding pigs. In the David story, a bit of geography helps to set the scene with the Philistines, and a Bible dictionary will help the storyteller translate "six cubits and a span."

While nearly all the Bible stories I tell are adaptions, two recent experiences have convinced me that the literal method deserves renewed attention in the church. The first experience was a conversation with several parishioners of a Roman Catholic church who had attended a mass celebrated by the bishop of Saginaw, Kenneth Untener. Bishop Untener memorizes the Gospel lesson as a part of his weekly preparation for preaching. During the service, rather than read the Gospel, he tells it. "It was as if I heard that passage for the first time," one friend told me. Another said, "I have never realized how powerful the bare words of the Scripture can be."

Many people think the bishop is adapting the lesson. He is frequently told, "I like the way you put the Bible into your own words." When he explains that what he did was to tell it word for word, they are amazed. Telling the gospel apparently makes it sound much more contemporary.

Later I had the opportunity to hear Professor Tom Boomershine tell a major section of The Gospel According to Mark word for word. Like my Michigan friends, I too listened as if the biblical events leaped from his mouth. I was transported back through the centuries and heard those stories as if I were inches from the events themselves. Though done simply, the telling was at once beautiful and powerful.

Why did this experience have such impact on me and on the others who listened? Some people suggest it is a matter of dynamics; the book no longer acts as a barrier between speaker and listener. Greater eye contact is possible.

I think the answer lies not just in the process but in the very nature of the Bible itself; it is an oral word. Telling is the Scripture's own special medium. When we tell the story, we open ourselves to the word's unique power. In the process we discover what Luther meant when he called the Bible a "word event" and the church a "mouth house" rather than a "pen house." Freed from its paper constraints, the word is communicated in its original form. Properly told, it is received with power.

People who are experienced in the literal method of biblical storytelling make several suggestions for those who wish to learn this ancient art. Begin by carefully studying the text, perhaps with the aid of a commentary. How you understand the passage will determine where you place the verbal accents. Next, select a good translation. Why spend long hours memorizing anything less than the most enduring language? For me, that would be the Revised Standard Version.

Since memorization is nearly a lost skill in our time, it is wise to carefully organize the process. First, divide the selection into shorter episodes, similar to the way you might outline. Proceed by reading the entire passage out loud 10 or 15 times. Since yours is an oral task, use an oral method. Finally, as much as possible, memorize phrase by phrase rather than word by word.

Although it is in its infant stages, there appears to be a resurgence of this basic kind of storytelling. The center may be United Theological Seminary in Dayton, Ohio, where Tom Boomershine teaches his New Testament students to memorize long sections of Scripture, particularly the passion and birth narratives. Although it may not be imminent, perhaps there will be a time when the people of God again will gather on a regular basis to hear the gospels told. That very process could help the church again become the people of the story.

Stories

David and the Golden Age

Nearly 1200 years before the birth of Christ, northern invaders drove people from their homes on Crete and in Asia Minor. These refugees wandered for a while, finally finding a place to live along the coastal plain of Palestine. The Philistines, or the "sea people" as they were called, quickly became a dominant force in that area of the Mediterranean. Their power was not derived from their number but by their development and use of an important new metal—iron!

Iron was used for swords, axe-heads, and chariots as well as ploughs and sickles. The possession of these powerful weapons of war soon kindled in them the desire to expand. With the

Mediterranean Sea on their western border, the Philistines naturally turned east toward the infant nation Israel.

Still organized into a loose confederation of tribes, the Israelites were no match for their powerful neighbors. One by one the 12 separate tribes were overwhelmed by the Philistine muscle, giving rise to a cry that the nation must develop a strong central government in order to withstand foreign aggression.

Although this idea eventually won acceptance, at first it was bitterly opposed by a strong minority led by the prophet Samuel. Ironically, it was this same Samuel who finally anointed the first king of Israel. His name—Saul.

Though Saul was a huge man possessing great ability, there was something tragic about this first king. Was it simply his lack of sensitivity to the voice of God, or was it because he was subject to deep depression—or are these two organically one?

In his early days, Saul was successful in his attempt to organize Israel against the Philistines. Later, as his jangled nerves left him more and more troubled, his son Jonathan arranged for a young shepherd to play simple melodies on his harp each evening at bedtime. This young boy quickly became a favorite of the moody king. The boy's name was David.

Soon, in an event unrelated to his role as court musician, the boy David went to visit his soldier brothers in the Shefelah foothills where they were engaged in battle with the Philistines. What David discovered was a pitiful sight. The Israelite soldiers were huddled in fear as a giant stood out on the plain shouting insults and challenging them to select one man to fight on their behalf—winner take all. David saw the challenge given not just to Israel, but to Israel's God. David accepted the challenge in the name of God, and the battle began.

The battle, however, was more than a fight between gods. It was a showdown between the latest in military might and simple primitive gallantry. The giant stood nine feet nine inches tall, or, if you prefer, six cubits and a span, and he was covered with the iron that had driven his nation to power. David, a mere boy, came before Goliath half-naked, with a slingshot and five smooth stones.

With one sure shot David hit the giant in an unprotected portion of the forehead and, when Goliath fell, cut off the giant's head with his own sword. Yahweh had shown forth his power; David became a hero.

From this point on, the story of David reads a bit like the conclusion of a fairy tale. The poor peasant boy returned to his king and was honored with the hand of the princess in marriage. He developed a strong and lasting friendship with the crown prince, Jonathan, and followed his victory over the giant with a number of impressive victories for the king. He was loved by the people.

One day, returning from battle in triumph, a chant arose from the people: "Saul has killed his thousands, but David his ten thousands." Though this was music to David's ears, it was hardly the kind of melody that an already-paranoid king needed to hear. Saul quickly turned against David.

One night, as David played for Saul, the melancholy king exploded, hurling a spear and barely missing his young friend. David fled from the room to his second-floor apartment with Saul's guards hot on his trail. The quick thinking of David's wife, Michal, who let him down from the window on a rope, saved his life. Though still deeply committed to his king, David was forced to flee to the hills.

Forced to live by his wits, David first found refuge at the sanctuary of Nob near Jerusalem, then later with Achish, the hated king of the Philistines. As time passed, a group of desperate men gathered around him, giving him a small private army. This guerrilla band made its living raiding foreign people and "protecting" farmers and people in small towns.

On several occasions while Saul was tracking him, David was able to slip inside the king's camp. Once David even entered the tent of his troubled friend, leaving a note to remind Saul that he could have killed him. David's loyalty to the king was a part of his religious faith. As long as Saul was the anointed of God, David could not touch the king, even in retaliation.

Finally, while David was serving as a border guard for the Philistines, both Saul and Jonathan were killed in battle. David grieved deeply for them both.

Shortly after the death of Saul, the already-fragile nation of Israel divided. Saul's son Ish-bosheth ruled the north, while the people of the south declared David as king. It was not long, however, before David defeated Ish-bosheth and brought the entire nation under his strong rule.

David was a remarkable man and a good king. His name, which means beloved, pointed to his great popularity with the people. A man of great character, David was sensitive and deeply honest. His love of music and poetry brought about a resurgence of art during his reign. He was a strong military leader, and under his reign Israel became a world power. There was a fairness about David that is pitifully lacking in most great leaders. He cared for the lame son of his dead friend Jonathan; he developed a system for sharing wealth with his personal troops.

Israel understood all of this in the light of David's deep devotion to God. It was Yahweh who was the source of Israel's strength. Under David Israel experienced a resurgence of piety.

David also was a man of strong emotions. He wept over the death of dear friends; he was moved to ecstasy when he was excited. In a poignant scene, as the ark of the covenant moved into Jerusalem, David danced wildly alongside the holy shrine, and in doing so he exposed a significant portion of his body. Michal, his wife, was offended, and she blistered him with her tongue, suggesting that he learn to act with the dignity expected from royalty. David was not impressed with Michal's opinions and told her that henceforth she would be sleeping alone.

David was a great man, but he was not without his dark side. His passion, for example, was not limited to fine music; he also collected wives. One day, while walking on his sun porch, looking down on his city, he saw a beautiful woman bathing. She was the wife of Uriah, a Hittite convert to Judaism and a soldier in David's army. Soon David and Bathsheba were involved in a torrid love affair, until Bathsheba became pregnant.

Bathsheba was deeply upset, and properly so, for adultery was punishable by death in Israel. Everyone was aware that her husband had been off fighting a war.

David quickly brought Uriah home in order to make it appear that he was the father of the child. However, David failed to account for the zeal of a convert. Uriah lived by the letter of the Jewish law, and the law clearly stated that no soldier shall sleep with a woman while involved in battle. By cracky, Uriah was not about to violate the oath of his profession and his new religion.

Since Uriah would not sleep with his wife, David sent him back to the front lines. His job, no doubt, was to lead the attack against a city under siege. In the battle, a giant boulder thrown over the side of the walled city killed Uriah. David and Bathsheba thought their problems were over. Unfortunately for both, Nathan the prophet could still count to nine.

One day Nathan visited the court of his king with a problem. "There were two men who lived in the same city, one rich, the other poor. The rich man had many sheep, the poor man had a single ewe lamb which he and his children raised as a household pet. When visitors came to the home of the rich man, instead of slaughtering one of his own flock, he took the lamb of the poor man and served it to his visitors."

David, a man with a great passion for justice, was incensed. "As the Lord lives, the man who has done this deserves to die!"

Nathan shot out his finger at David and said, "You are that man! Why do you despise the word of the Lord? The sword will never leave from your house because you have despised me, says the Lord. I will raise up evil against you out of your own house."

It was a dark moment, a moment of great despair for David. Indeed he *was* the man. Unlike other kings, this one knew that he answered to one greater than himself, Yahweh. David accepted Nathan's pronouncement and God's judgment and repented. The spirit of that repentance is found in Psalm 51.

Though he repented, judgment did come. It was served

through jealous wives and their spoiled offspring. It came through haughty, headstrong sons. David's son Amnon raped Tamar, his half-sister. Later Absalom, another of David's sons, avenged his sister's disgrace by killing Amnon. Absalom was banished by his father into the wilderness, though he was allowed to return later. Back in the royal court, Absalom organized a revolt against the aging king, and, caught off guard, David was forced to flee from Jerusalem, again claiming the wilderness as his sanctuary. There, with his great military leader, Joab, he made plans to regain the throne. David gave explicit orders to Joab not to harm the boy. Instead, when the opportunity arose, Joab killed Absalom. As David wept over the death of his rebellious son, the words of Nathan echoed through his mind.

David was a great king and a great military leader. Under him Israel lived through its golden age; never again would it enjoy the power and prestige that it possessed under the former singing shepherd. Israel has waited for nearly 3000 years, dreaming of a return to the greatness it experienced under David.

David—musician, soldier, poet, humanitarian, pious and devout king. He ruled Israel for 40 years, and Solomon, son of Bathsheba, succeeded him on the throne.

Daniel and His Friends

Nearly 600 years before the birth of Christ, the armies of Babylon marched into Judah destroying every fortified city and leaving the temple in Jerusalem in ruins. Judah's leaders, the strong, healthy, and capable who were not killed or who did not escape, were taken captive back to Babylon. It was a disaster of tremendous proportions. Only the poorest peasants, those considered incapable of causing trouble, were allowed to remain in Judah to harvest the crops.

Though the Jews who were taken to Babylon were allowed some freedom, including the right to gather together, life was not easy. Gone was temple worship. Gone was Jewish culture. The poet describes the difficulty of life in exile in Psalm 137:

By the waters of Babylon, there we sat down and wept,
when we remembered Zion.
On the willows there we hung up our lyres.
For there our captors required of us songs,
and our tormentors, mirth, saying,
"Sing us one of the songs of Zion!"
How shall we sing the Lord's song in a foreign land?
If I forget you, O Jerusalem, let my right hand wither!
Let my tongue cleave to the roof of my mouth,
if I do not remember you,
if I do not set Jerusalem above my highest joy!

It was a great struggle to remain Jewish in Babylon. It was difficult to maintain the Jewish faith in the face of all of the secular influences and the strong ties to other religions. Many were lost; some became secular Jews. There were some that did not waver, however. It is these hardy ones that the book of Daniel extolls.

Among those who were brought from Jerusalem to Babylon were a group of bright young men, born of nobility and well educated. They were assigned to the king's own training school for a three-year course. Daniel, whom the king later renamed Belteshazzar, Shadrach, Meshach, and Abednego, four friends, were a part of that group.

The initial test for the four young men was the food served by the king's cooks. It was not kosher. If they ate the rich food, they would be breaking Jewish dietary laws and defiling themselves. Daniel pleaded with the chef, "Please don't make us eat this food."

The chef responded, "I fear lest my lord the king, who appointed your food and your drink, should see that you are in poorer condition than the other men."

"Why not test us for 10 days," Daniel countered. "Let us eat vegetables and drink water while the others are fed the king's rich food. At the end, observe our health yourself." The chef agreed to such a test, and when the 10 days had passed it was clear that Daniel and his friends were better in appearance than those who ate the king's food. From that day on, Daniel and his friends were allowed to eat only food that was kosher. A blow was struck for the religious law (and for health foods).

Later, when Daniel was able to interpret a dream whose meaning evaded all the wise men of the court, he won favor with the ruler. Impressed with Daniel's ability to help him not only remember what he dreamed, but to also interpret it, the king declared, "Your God is God of gods and Lord of kings, and a revealer of mysteries. . . ." It was a short-lived conversion, as we shall soon see. Daniel and his friends rose in stature; Shadrach, Meshach, and Abednego were placed over the affairs of the province of Babylon, while Daniel remained in the king's court.

Shortly after his confession of faith, the king assembled all the satraps, prefects, governors, counselors, treasurers, justices, magistrates, and all the officials of the provinces to the dedication of an image of gold, sixty cubits by six cubits in size. "You are commanded," the king declared, "when you hear the sound of the horn, pipe, lyre, trigon, harp, and bagpipe, to fall down and worship the golden image that I have set up. Whoever does not fall down and worship shall immediately be cast into a burning fiery furnace."

True to the king's edict, when the sound of the horn, pipe, lyre, trigon, harp, and bagpipe was heard, *all* people, of every tongue and nation, fell down and worshiped the golden image. All except for a few religious Jews—such as Shadrach, Meshach, and Abednego. Soon their refusal to bow down and worship the golden image was reported to the king who brought the three before his court and demanded them to answer the charge against them.

Shadrach, Meshach, and Abednego listened to the king's charges and replied, "O Nebuchadnezzar, we have no need to answer you in this matter. If it be so, our God whom we serve is able to deliver us from the burning fiery furnace; and he will deliver us out of your hand, O king. But if not, be it known to you, O king, that we will not serve your gods or worship the golden image which you have set up."

Then Nebuchadnezzar was full of fury, and the expression of his face was changed against the three men. He ordered the furnace heated seven times more than normal, and he ordered Shadrach, Meshach, and Abednego to be cast into the fiery furnace. They were bound in their mantles, their tunics, their hats, and their other garments, and they were cast into the burning fiery furnace. The flame was so hot that it killed the men who took the three Jews to the furnace.

When the king rose up, he said to the counselors, "Did we not cast three men into the fire?" They answered, "True, O king." "But," he gasped, "I see four men loose, walking in the midst of the fire, and they are not hurt; and the appearance of the fourth is like a son of the gods."

Then the king went to the furnace and ordered the three out, and all gathered around them and saw that the fire had not any power over the bodies of the men. Their hair was not singed, their mantles were not harmed. And Nebuchadnezzar said, "Blessed be the God of Shadrach, Meshach, and Abednego, who has sent his angel and delivered his servants, who trusted in him, and set at nought the king's command. I will therefore make a decree, those who speak against the God of Shadrach, Meshach, and Abednego shall be torn limb from limb, and their houses laid in ruins; for there is no other god who is able to deliver in this way."

When Nebuchadnezzar died, his son Belshazzar succeeded him. Later Belshazzar was overthrown by Darius the Mede. Daniel and his three friends continued to serve all of the kings faithfully.

Now Darius liked Daniel, and he promoted him above all other presidents and satraps because "an excellent spirit was in him." Eventually the king planned to have Daniel rule over the whole kingdom. Other officials were jealous of Daniel's success and decided to set him up.

Going to the king, the presidents and satraps said, "O King

Darius, live forever! We are all agreed that for 30 days you should establish an ordinance and enforce an interdict, that whoever makes petition to any god or man except to you shall be cast into the den of lions." Darius, pleased with their suggestions, signed the document and the interdict.

Though Daniel knew about the document, he continued to pray before the open windows in his upper chambers which faced Jerusalem three times a day, giving thanks to God. After watching Daniel at prayer for several days, the presidents and satraps went before the king and asked, "Is your order still valid?"

The king answered, "It is!"

"Then," they cried, "Daniel, one of the exiles from Judah, pays no heed to you and continues to make his petitions three times a day."

The king was greatly distressed, but he declared that the law of the Medes and Persians stood. He reluctantly brought Daniel to the lions' den and declared, "May your God, whom you serve continually, deliver you." A stone was sealed upon the mouth of the lions' den, and the king went to his palace where he spent a restless night. At the break of day, the king arose and went quickly to the den of lions, crying out, "O Daniel, servant of the living God, has your God, whom you serve continually, been able to deliver you from the lions?"

Daniel replied, "O king, live forever! My God sent his angel and shut the lions' mouths, and they have not hurt me, because I was found blameless before him; and also before you, O king, I have done no wrong."

Then, at the king's command, Daniel was taken up out of the den and found to be unhurt. In his place his accusers were cast into the den of lions with their wives and children. Before they reached the bottom, the lions overpowered them.

King Darius declared to all the people: "I make a decree that in all my royal dominion all tremble and fear before the God of Daniel, for he is the living God, enduring forever; his kingdom shall never be destroyed, and his dominion shall be to the end. He delivers and rescues, he works signs and wonders in heaven and on earth, he who has saved Daniel from the power of the lions."

The king had learned what Daniel and his friends had known all along—kings of the earth come and go, but the Lord reigns forever.

The Prodigal Son

Once there was a man who had two sons. The younger came to his wealthy father and said, "Father, give me my share of the inheritance." The father divided his living between the two boys. Soon after that the son left his Jewish home and traveled to a far country where he squandered his property in loose living. When he had spent his last dollar, a famine arose in that country, and he began to feel the pinch. In desperation he hired himself out to a Gentile farmer, one who neither observed the Sabbath nor the dietary laws. The job he was given was tending pigs. As he fed the animals, he remembered an ancient saying, "Cursed is he who feeds swine." He was indeed alone in a strange land. He was so hungry he would have happily eaten pig food. Then he came to his senses and said to himself, "Why, at home my father's servants have plenty to eat, but I am nearly starving. I will arise and go to my father and say to him, 'Father, I have sinned against heaven and before you; I am not worthy to be called your son; treat me as one of your hired servants.' " Immediately he began the long journey home. While he was still a long ways away his father rose and did something very undignified—he ran! When he reached his son, he hugged and kissed him, not on the hand, like a slave, but on the head, like a son.

Now the older son was still in the fields. As he came home he heard music. Calling to one of the servants, he asked what was happening. The servant said, "Your brother has come home and your father has killed a fatted calf, because he has received him safe and sound."

Angry and upset, the older brother refused to go in. His father, sensing something was wrong, came out and urged him to join the party. In an outburst he shouted, "All these years I have faithfully served you, never disobeying, and yet you never gave me a calf that I might party with my friends. But when this, this son of yours who has squandered your money on whores come home, you kill the fatted calf!"

The father reached out to his son and said gently, "Son, you are always with me. Don't you know that all I own is yours? It seemed only fitting to celebrate, for your brother was dead, and is alive; he was lost, and is found."

5

Stories for Christmas

Christmas itself is a story and as such invites us into a season that abounds with marvelous tales. Like the incarnation, good Christmas stories are full of deep emotions and mystery. They speak of unexpected joy interrupting the lives of common folks and the excitement of self-giving, and they provoke a sense of awe, wonder, and appreciation. This season, more than any other, seems to encourage writers and storytellers to create enchanting tales.

There are, of course, as many unusable stories for the Christmas storyteller as ones of quality. Many Christmas tales, including a host of the made-for-TV variety, seem to be almost totally lacking in substance. What they lack in plot, they attempt to make up with cute gimmicks. One of those gimmicks is to include animals in the story. Still other stories seem to be characterized more by hocus-pocus than by what Christians refer to as mystery.

Storytellers in the church must look carefully at the message of the gospel and decide which tales are compatible with the story of the incarnation of our Lord and which are not. Thus, for this storyteller, tales about Santa Claus are out, though stories of St. Nicholas are clearly usable. On a Sunday close to December 6, St. Nicholas Day, it is fitting to tell children of all ages the story of this great Christian saint. It may be best to let listeners know that the legend of St. Nicholas can no longer be separated from the events of his life before proceeding to tell his story.

The prime story of the Christmas season, of course, is found in the gospels of St. Matthew and St. Luke. Though there is great beauty in reading the Christmas narrative, telling it is extremely effective. In either reading or telling, the greatest obstacle in communication is the story's familiarity. Preparation is the key to overcoming this problem.

The storyteller must begin the preparation by paying close attention to the stage directions found within the text itself. Next, observe the emotions of the actors—fear, joy, amazement, pensiveness, and resignation are most obvious. Two of these words, *amazement* and *fear*, form an almost repetitive theme. The emotion and rhythm as outlined in Matthew and Luke shapes the telling. One's voice, hands, and eyes all reflect the spirit of the story.

Finally, the storyteller must carefully select the language used for the telling. Since it is almost impossible to improve on the original, the storyteller should either memorize the familiar story or stay very close to the text, utilizing the strong images found in either the Revised Standard version or the King James version rather than the more pallid language of the modern translations.

Resources for Christmas Stories

Most public libraries will have at least one book of Christmas stories. Two of the better collections are *The Way of*

Christmas by Ruth Sawyer and *Stories of Christ and Christmas* edited by Edward Wagenknecht. (Please see the bibliography at the end of this book for a more complete listing of resources including publishers.)

There are a number of traditional Christmas stories that can be used during this season. O. Henry's "The Gift of the Magi," Hans Christian Anderson's "The Fir Tree'" and "The Little Match Girl," and Beatrix Potter's "The Tailor of Gloucester" are particularly enjoyable stories.

Legend has it that St. Francis was the first to have a Christmas creche, using *real* animals. Found in the stories and legends of St. Francis, this tale is most appropriate on Christmas Eve.

Though Leo Tolstoy's famous tale "Where Love Is, God Is" is appropriate at any time of the year, it is frequently used at Christmas. This classic story has a counterpart in nearly every language. Ruth Sawyer tells a Spanish version while Edwin Markham's poem is called "How the Great Guest Came." In each version, a poor but pious person expects Jesus to visit his home. Though the preparations are complete, only needy strangers appear at the door. At the end, the one who waits for the coming of Jesus understands the truth of Matthew 25, that what we do for others, we do for Jesus.

A few years ago a story by Martin Bell in his collection *The Way of the Wolf* became quite popular. The story, "Barrington Bunny," is the tale of a rabbit finding the meaning of community and sacrifice during a snowstorm on Christmas Eve. "Barrington" has been adapted by some churches for use in their church school programs, using children to act out the story. I have used it during children's Christmas Eve services.

Stories

The Juggler of God

This is my adaption of a 700-year-old French tale. Anatole France used it as the basis of a short story. Massenet made it into an opera. Retold in English by Ruth Sawyer, John Harrell, Barbara Cooney, and most recently in a colorful children's book by Tomie De Paola, Barnaby appears variously as a young boy or an old man. My version differs from the others mentioned primarily by placing the story in the United States.

The New Orleans streets were packed with tourists desperate for a good time. They hurried down Bourbon Street stopping at each bar long enough to hear the sweet sounds of Dixieland flowing into the early evening air. Barkers ventured outside barroom doors to invite men and women in to witness the dancers.

On Jackson Square women sat as still as statues as the artists carefully etched their portraits—for $35 a sitting. At nearly every street corner minstrels performed for anyone who would stop to listen, hoping to be rewarded with a few coins. There were flutists, guitarists, and mandolin players, and, of course, the inevitable scores of young black children dancing. The spirit of Mardi Gras was in the air, and the crowd was in a joyous mood. The musicians knew that meant a good evening for them.

Quietly, on a not-so-busy corner, an old man, slightly bent over, was setting up for his show. The battered sign that was set against a light pole read: The Great Barnaby—Juggler. On a small stand a suitcase lay open, filled with knives, pins, and an assortment of balls, all tools of the juggler's trade.

In his prime Barnaby had been on all of the great stages in America. Once he had even traveled with a group to England, where he performed for the queen. Not only could Barnaby do the conventional tricks of the juggler using pins, knives, and keeping seven balls in the air, but his repertoire also included a show-stopper. At the conclusion of the act, he would lie on his hands, face downward, while he threw five golden balls into the air, juggling them with his feet.

All of that was in his prime. Unable to do his greatest tricks, Barnaby now appeared only on street corners before the fickle eyes of tourists. When the night was over, there was barely enough in the coin box to pay the rent. Many nights there was not enough in his pockets for even a hamburger. Hunger was no stranger to Barnaby.

"Tonight will be different," he thought. "The crowd is in a festive mood; tonight they will be generous."

Without even an introduction, the old vaudeville man began his show. First the pins. He began with three and slowly added more until the number reached six. A small crowd began to gather, and they applauded politely when he finished. Next the small balls. At one time he could toss them between his legs and catch them behind his back. Tonight he was happy to keep them in the air in a conventional manner.

As Barnaby began the more difficult feats, he was aware that his timing was not good. "Perhaps," he thought, 'it is because the stomach is empty." Twice he tried to get the knives into the air, but they refused to cooperate and dropped to the ground. The crowd laughed and began to break up.

Desperately Barnaby spoke. "Ladies and gentlemen, you are about to witness one of the most difficult and amazing juggling feats in the world." People stopped as the old man placed his frame in a prone position and began his most famous trick. Clearly it was a gamble, for he had not done the trick in years. Alas, the feet this night were no more cooperative than his hands. Twice the balls fell to the ground, and before he could begin again, the crowd was on its way. Barnaby's coin box was empty.

The old man sat on his suitcase and looked forlornly at the hands that had betrayed him. Thirty years passed before his eyes as he dreamed of the glory and applause that were once his.

Then a voice brought Barnaby back to the present. "Things

didn't go so well for you tonight, my man." The old trouper looked up to see the shining eyes of a man dressed in black.

"I am Father Maurice from St. Helen's parish. I have watched you at Mass each morning. I can tell by your eyes and your manner when you receive the blessed sacrament that you love the Lord. I have also watched you perform on this street corner during the past few weeks." The kind priest smiled. "Barnaby, I have come with an offer."

Quietly he told the juggler that there was a place for him on the staff of a monastery not far from the city. "The pay is horrible, but the food is good, the beds are warm, and you will live with brothers in Christ."

That is how Barnaby the Great came to live at the monastery, not far from the heart of New Orleans. He quickly discovered that Father Maurice's assessment of life there was accurate. The food was delicious, the beds comfortable, and though his companions were men of few words, he began to feel like he was part of a family.

Barnaby's work was primarily cleaning floors and assisting with the evening meal. This labor contrasted greatly with that of the other brothers who were primarily artists of one kind or another. Brother James was a carver of great talent, Brother Lawrence an organist and composer. Others were writers, painters, or weavers. Only the work of Brother Richard, the cook, was similar. Working together in the kitchen, the two men became fast friends.

More than anything else, Barnaby enjoyed worship. He had always been a devout man. Now life in the monastery allowed him ample time for prayer and adoration of the Christ. Barnaby was a contented man.

As summer turned to fall, and fall to winter, Barnaby grew more accustomed to his new home. With Christmas approaching, however, he became a bit disturbed. There was an air of expectation in the monastery that he did not share. Brother James was busy finishing a new carving that would be unveiled on Christmas Eve. Brother Lawrence was working on an original cantata that would be performed by a nearby seminary chorus. Even Richard, the cook, seemed to have a sudden burst of energy, baking for the festive season.

One day while they were preparing supper, Barnaby shared his concern with his friend. "Everyone here has a special gift that adds to the holy season. I alone am without a single thing that can be given to the Christ child on the day of his birth."

"There are many ways to serve Christ, dear friend," the cook replied. "My special soups and tarts are done to his glory. The gardener grows beautiful flowers as his act of worship. Why, it was St. Francis who said that everything sings of the glory of God. You clean floors and make certain that the dishes are spotless. These are like great frescos in the eyes of God."

Barnaby thought about the words of his friend that night. Certainly St. Francis was correct, but somehow clean floors did not seem gift enough on the night of the Christ's birth.

As he took his place in the chapel for evening prayer, Barnaby's eyes fell on the only thing that disturbed him about this beautiful room. Near the altar stood a marble statue of the blessed mother and her child. Both seemed so sad. Each time he looked at the statue, he remembered the laughter that he had brought people for nearly 30 years. "It is too bad someone can't bring a gift of laughter to the Christ child," he thought.

As he rose and returned to his room, a marvelous idea came to him. Quickly he walked to his bed and pulled out the old suitcase. It had lain untouched since he had entered the monastery nine months before. He looked down at the copper balls and fingered them gently. "Just a little practice each day," he thought, "and the touch will return. There is yet time; Christmas is still a week away."

His chores were performed quickly the next day in order that he could return to his room to test his skill. The following days were the same.

On Christmas Eve Brother James displayed his statue in the

chapel for the first time. It was stunning. During the Christmas mass the choir performed a selection from the wonderful new work by Brother Lawrence. It was a perfect evening.

When it appeared that all had retired to their rooms, Barnaby, suitcase in hand, crept quietly back into the chapel. After bowing before the statue of the Christ, he carefully arranged his equipment in the order in which it would be used.

First the pins. Next the seven copper balls. As he tossed them in the air, they caught the light of the candles and sparkled with a rainbow of colors. It was years since he had performed so well.

Just as he began with the knives, one of the brothers passed by and saw the old man at work. Alarmed, he ran to bring the prior to witness the sacrilege. He, in turn, brought two others from the order with him.

Barnaby had concluded his knife routine by the time the brothers had gathered silently in the doorway. Now what they witnessed was the old man lying face down, in front of the altar, juggling six copper balls with his feet. It was an amazing performance.

To the brothers, however, it was an act of shame. Nodding silently to each other, they began to move forward to remove him from the chapel. Surely Barnaby had been seized with madness.

Before they moved but a few steps, Brother Richard held his hand in the air and pointed to the marble statue. What they saw was the Christ child gleefully clapping his hands and the Virgin applauding.

"Everything sings of the glory of God," the cook whispered to the gathered assembly.

The prior nodded and responded, "God be praised," and silently retreated to his room.

A Legend for Christmas
Similar to "Where Love Is, God Is" by Leo Tolstoy, this German legend that I have adapted picks up on a theme found fre-

quently in stories about Christ—those who meet Jesus often find him in the faces of the poor.

In a large midwestern city, a little child wandered through the streets on Christmas Eve gazing at the busy people rushing back and forth, arms filled with presents. Everyone seemed happy. Everyone seemed to have a destination. Everyone except the little child.

As he walked, the bitter cold nipped at his cheeks and bit at his bare fingers. This was no night to be out alone. He must find a place to stay.

He turned down a boulevard dotted with large homes, the kind where the yards are imprisoned by iron fences. Mustering his courage, he walked to the door of a very attractive house and peered through the curtains at the gaily decorated Christmas tree. Inside the house, the children were playing hide and seek, though they paused every now and then to shake presents that had their names on them.

The little child stood on tiptoe and pushed the button that rang the bell. Soon a tall boy opened the door and gazed down at the youngster. "I am sorry," he said. "Our father is not home, and he would not like to have anyone upset our Christmas Eve." The door closed slowly, almost apologetically.

The little child soon tried another home. This time a stout woman shouted at him, "Get off our property, and I mean now!"

The wind seemed as angry as the woman when the young child reached the unsheltered sidewalk. He decided to try a street where the houses were a bit smaller, hoping the people were more friendly. On this street he was greeted by a woman who was afraid he would bring germs into the house and a father who said there wasn't enough even for his own children. But mostly he was greeted by silence. People simply looked at him, shook their heads, and sadly closed the door.

"There must be some place in this great city for me," he thought, as he stumbled through the dark streets. Now he passed houses with fewer lights, houses much smaller in size.

At the end of the street, he stopped at a small cottage with no curtains. It was easy to see into this tiny home. On a table sat a small tree without lights. Near the fireplace a mother read to her two small children. Her daughter sat on her lap, while her son snuggled close to her feet.

"Mommy," the little girl cried out, interrupting the reading. "Someone is at the door."

"It is just the trees," the boy assured them.

Before the mother could continue, the noise was heard again, and all of them rushed to the door to see what had made the sound. There in the doorway stood a little child, shaking in the cold.

The mother picked him up and pressed him tightly to her breast, even as she carried him to the living room. "Quickly, warm some milk," she called to her son as she rubbed the numbed fingers between her hands. Pushing his tangled hair back, she tenderly kissed the child on the forehead and whispered, "We are delighted that you have come to share our Christmas with us."

For nearly an hour the four stood around the fire until feeling began to return to the frozen body of the little stranger. When their guest seemed to be warmed, the little girl said, "Finish the story, Mommy." Agreeing, the mother placed the little girl on her lap and opened the book.

Suddenly a powerful light began to flood the room. The small family turned to see the little child transformed before their eyes. The light from his face became so bright that they were forced to turn their heads. Then the light left the room, and, as the family rushed to the door, they watched him ascend until all that was visible was a star that shone brilliantly over their home, bathing the entire area in light.

The boy was the first to break the silence. "Was it the Christ child, Mother?" he asked.

"Yes," she said simply.

It is said that each Christmas God sends his Son wandering through the streets of some city in our land, seeking a place to be warmed. When he is accepted, God sends a star of brilliant light to shine. This Christmas, look around you for those in need, and look up, dear friends, to see God's sign.

A Refugee Christmas

This story is dedicated to the people in American churches who have opened their doors and their hearts to the flood of refugees. It was written for Christmas 1979.

Daniel wasn't much of a pastor, but then, he didn't have much of a congregation either. At 55 his energy level, which had never been very high, was ebbing noticeably. It was his lackadaisical past that had caused the bishop to "strongly urge" him to move to Cedarville. Actually there wasn't much choice; he had resigned from North Prairie in September, and with Christmas coming he needed an income again.

In November Daniel had loaded a small U-Haul with his meager bachelor belongings and driven the 90 miles to Our Savior's Church. There were the inevitable cartons of books, a sofa, some bedroom furniture, a La-Z-Boy rocker, a few dishes, his beloved organ, and three TV sets. Only the organ and the TV sets bear further mention.

Daniel had worked his way through college and seminary by playing the organ. Though he no longer played professionally, he continued to receive requests to play at installations and social gatherings of his church.

If the organ was for public display, the TV sets belonged to Daniel's hidden side. He was a TV addict. He watched nearly anything that came over the airwaves — soaps, game shows, and late-night movies as well as all of the prime-time shows. A small set was placed on top of a console in order that he could watch two programs at once. The third, like the alcoholic's hidden bottle, was insurance.

Now firmly settled in Cedarville, the new pastor was aware that the congregation was seriously split into two groups: a small group of mostly younger families who had rallied around the former pastor and a much larger group, primarily older people, who resisted attempts to modernize Our Savior's.

Daniel, never one to rock the boat, assured the church council at its first meeting that he preferred the old liturgy, the traditional hymns, and that he didn't have a single new program in mind for the congregation. The men applauded. Our Savior's Church, Cedarville, would remain a bulwark against a changing world.

It had not been so when Pastor DeSota had been there. Fresh out of seminary, the young pastor came full of new ideas. One Christmas Eve the congregation had worshiped in a barn, and the people were asked to sing "Mary had a little lamb, he was the lamb of God" to the tune of the nursery rhyme. When he left abruptly, utterly frustrated, the younger people in the congregation cried, while the older folks heaved a collective sigh of relief.

As the days moved into early December, it was evident that the rift in the congregation was very serious. The division began affecting businesses and families, and some even spoke of finding another church home, an unheard-of alternative for people in that small community.

Since Daniel wasn't sure what to do about the situation, he did nothing. He continued to visit shut-ins, attend a few meetings, write his sermons, and still find plenty of time to watch TV.

On the 17th of December, the phone rang, and the voice at the other end said, "This is Marie from Immigration and Refugee Services. I want to confirm the arrival of your Cambodian family on the 19th. They leave Hong Kong tomorrow morning and will arrive at your airport Monday at 11:22 A.M."

Silence greeted the woman from Daniel's end of the line. "Are you certain you have the correct party?" he finally managed to mumble.

"Is this Our Savior's Church, Cedarville?"

"Yes."

"Sir, I have several pieces of correspondence with Pastor DeSota, one as late as November 3."

Why he didn't tell the nice woman that it was all a terrible mistake and that she would just have to find someone else to house the family, he didn't know. But he didn't.

For five minutes after he hung up, Daniel sat in shock. Then he made two phone calls, confirming a hunch. The arrival of the six southeast Asian refugees was not a total surprise to everyone. A few of the younger families had been consulted, though everyone assumed that the former pastor had "canceled the order" when he left abruptly in November.

On Sunday evening Daniel called a meeting at the church to decide what to do. The basement was packed. At first the group was split along predictable lines. Friends of the former pastor insisted that if people hadn't made life so miserable for DeSota, they wouldn't be in this mess. The others, equally vociferous, argued that this was typical of the former pastor, going off half-cocked, making all kinds of plans without consulting anyone. No one seemed thrilled over the prospect of locating a family just a few days before Christmas.

The meeting was approaching its second hour before one of the older members asked Daniel what he thought. Until that moment he had remained silent, his normal behavior in the face of controversy.

"There is a great deal about this situation that I don't understand," he began. "What I do know is this: tomorrow morning six human beings, through no fault of their own, will be arriving at the airport without food, clothing, housing, or friends. A Wisconsin winter is hard enough to face under the best of circumstances." He paused for a moment before concluding. "I intend to be at that airport tomorrow. I intend to be their friend. Do any of you plan to help?"

After a moment of silence, the room nearly exploded with excitement. No longer did people begin their sentences with "*If* this family comes"; instead they said "*When* they come. . . ." In the next 90 minutes, committees were formed to find food and clothing, and a woman in her 80s, one of the former pastor's most vocal critics, offered her house to the family until a permanent residence could be found.

Later that evening, Daniel fell exhausted into his bed, pleased with what had happened but still apprehensive about what was to come.

The next morning the welcoming committee was nearly to the airport before it dawned on them that they would not be able to understand a single word this family would say. As it turned out, they need not have worried even that long. When the family of six—a mother and father in their mid-30s, two girls, 12 and 11, a boy, 4, and a grandmother—stepped off the plane, they communicated wonderfully in the universal language of gesture—smiles, handshakes, and even a tentative hug.

The next five days were hectic. The phone rang constantly. People offered food, clothing, and transportation. On Tuesday a house was located that needed fixing, and several volunteers quickly stepped forward to begin the necessary repairs. On Wednesday a pickup pulled into the church parking lot, filled with furniture. On Thursday an interpreter was found. One of the young men coming home from college brought an international student with him. At last people would not be limited to pantomime for communication.

In all of the activity Daniel noticed a strange phenomenon. Side by side on the committees and work crews, supporters of former Pastor DeSota labored with those who could not wait to get rid of the man.

Late Friday night, as he climbed into bed, Daniel realized that his TV sets had sat idle for the last six days. As he concluded his evening prayers, he also remembered that he had not prepared for tomorrow night's Christmas Eve service. Daniel, who normally read a manuscript, had not written a single word for his sermon. Another time that would have been cause for panic, but tonight he was too tired.

On Saturday, December 24, Our Savior's Church, normally reserved and silent, was buzzing. People who ordinarily entered quietly and sat in their pews until worship began were in the aisles talking and shaking hands. No one even noticed when the organist began her prelude.

At precisely 8:00 the church grew quiet, not because the acolyte had lit the candles or the choir had begun the processional, but because six tiny people, led by an 80-year-old woman, had entered the church and found their way to the very front pew, right under the elevated pulpit.

When the service began, the church nearly shook with the singing. No one could remember such a display of enthusiasm at worship. Daniel seemed to beam clear up to the time the choir sang the anthem. The sermon, still unprepared, was next.

As he mounted the steps to the pulpit, Daniel was surprised at how calm he felt. As he read the Christmas Gospel, his voice had a ring that was not ordinarily there. When he finished the beautiful story from the second chapter of Luke, he paused before he began to speak.

"Dear friends. A great deal has happened in this church in the past few days. In a way it is very much like the story of the first Christmas, where room was discovered for our Lord on the night of his birth, a night when he and his family were refugees. Many things have happened that have helped me to hear this story as if it were very new. Do you feel that way too?" Heads seemed to nod in response.

"We must not think that this Christmas is more meaningful because we suddenly have become generous people. That is like saying if we would all try just a little harder, this world would be a better place to live. That is, of course, what many people think the Christmas message is all about. Try a little harder. Love a little more.

"But that is not the Christmas message. Left to our own ways, we would remain a divided and separated people. Left to our own goodness, our Christmas would be as drab as it has been in the past. No, what has happened is that God has broken into our lives just as he broke into the lives of a people nearly 2000 years ago. With a phone call and the arrival of six strangers, our God has interrupted our plans and schemes and brought us together. This bringing together—we call it reconciliation—is what the coming of Jesus is all about. Because he has come we are no longer strangers or enemies, we are friends —and it is his doing."

Daniel fought the impulse to continue. He had already said more than he intended. Instead, he looked at them—and saw them. Then he concluded, "God bless you all."

Following the benediction, Daniel moved to the narthex to greet people, a task he normally dreaded. Tonight, however, he cherished the opportunity to greet friends. As they met, he was nearly overcome with the warm wishes from "his" people.

When the long line finally passed, Daniel returned to the sanctuary. There, with the interpreter, stood the six new residents of Cedarville. "The family has been practicing a greeting," the young student said, "in English."

With this the father bowed and spoke clearly. "Thank you for giving us a home." Though he could not remember the last time he cried in the presence of another person, tears now rolled down Daniel's cheeks.

After he dried his eyes and cleared his throat, the pastor said, "Please tell these lovely people that we are quite even. We have given them a home—and they have given us a Christmas."

6

Folktales, Fables, and Legends

It is a rare and unfortunate child who has not been introduced to folktales and fairy stories during the formative years. Filled with nasty dragons and evil stepmothers, these tales capture the attention of children, leaving them breathless, awaiting the happy ending.

Though the major attraction of these stories is their fascinating plots, it is clear that there is a lot of learning going on while the tale is told. Through these ancient tales, we have handed down noble virtues, folk wisdom, and human resources to face life's most difficult questions.

The fairy story also addresses those inner conflicts that we face during our early years. Sibling rivalry ("Cinderella"), parental jealousy ("Snow White"), and sexuality ("The Frog and the Princess") are but a few of the subjects that are approached through these stories, not in lecture form, but in the impressionable language of symbol.

Deeply spiritual, the fairy story is a splendid resource for the Christian storyteller. Like the parables of Jesus, however, these stories do not talk directly about God. Rather, their secular message is that pride and avarice are punished while gentleness and humility are rewarded. In the end, the listener is left confident that the future is secure. In similar fashion to the stories of Jesus, we see a battle raging between the kingdom of the meek and the forces of arrogance and power.

Though far from identical, the world of the fairy tale and the world of the gospel both recognize that the dark forces of this world are real, that they are armed with a power that brings suffering and pain to existence. This part of the message is lost, of course, if we cover up the cruelty and death of the stories, as is the custom of Walt Disney. In these "cleaned-up" versions, foolishness is not fatal. Gone is the sense of judgment, the message that we suffer the consequences of our sins. It seems both unnecessary and absurd to attempt to protect children from the horrors of life. Through fantasy they can imagine situations that are much worse than the ones in these ancient stories. If we are willing to face the tragedy of the story, through frequent telling the listener begins to gain a confidence that, in spite of bad times, the future is secure.

It is in their endings that the gospel story and the fairy story come close. Both end with a sense of hope. Both, J. R. R. Tolkien maintains, tell of a world that ends happily ever after. Both declare that joy happens. In both worlds it is a marvelous grace from beyond us that rescues us from the dangers of this world.

Tolkien is quick to say that the Christian joy, the *gloria,* is of the purest kind. It is infinitely high and joyous, overwhelming the message of the fairy story. Frederick Buechner has echoed Tolkien: "That is the fairy tale of the Gospel with, of course, the one crucial difference from all other fairy tales, which is that the claim made for it is that it is true, that it not only happened once upon a time, but has kept on happening ever since and is happening still."

A second type of stories that arises out of the folktale genre is the fable. Unlike the fairy tale, whose major purpose is to delight, the fable is a teaching story. Each fable carries a message or lesson, though the little morals at the end of Aesop's fables appear to be later additions.

Dominated by animals in order to more easily classify character types (crafty, foolish, brave), the fable has left us with a treasure of sayings that have become a part of folk wisdom: "Don't count your chickens before they hatch," "a wolf in sheep's clothing," "sour grapes," and "a dog in the manger" are a few examples.

For Christians the fables are best understood as a kind of wisdom literature—as proverbs. Some have even suggested that proverbs are short fables.

Resources for Folktales

Most libraries have copies of *Aesop's Fables* in one form or another. Those interested in the relationship between the fable and the Christian message will enjoy *Aesop and the Bible* by Alison and Trevor Morrison.

Most fairy stories can be found in collections. Some, like the tales of the Brothers Grimm and Hans Christian Andersen, are relatively easy to locate. Note that most books have but a few of the many stories collected by the Grimms. Perhaps the most complete collection of ancient folktales in the English language is the 12-volume collection *The Fairy Books* by Andrew Lang. It is a rare library that has this set, though most can borrow it for you.

Most of us simply have to go to our local libraries and search through the folktale section to find what is available. After we find a usable story, we generally will have to adapt it for oral use. Some collections, such as ones by Virginia Haviland, Ruth Sawyer, or Marie Shedlock, are already in oral form.

I have made no attempt to adapt the stories of J. R. R. Tolkien, though I enjoy reading them aloud. C. S. Lewis' tales are more usable for me. I have used sections of his books and have even told an entire book, *Perelandra.*

Jewish folktales are extremely valuable. Many of them have a biblical slant already and are easily adapted for use in the church. The two-volume work by Martin Buber, *Tales of the Hasidim,* and *Souls on Fire* by Elie Wiesel are collections of Hasidic stories and sayings. Wiesel has also compiled aspects of the Midrash into his helpful book *Messengers of God.*

Often beautiful tales are found in single volumes in the children's section of the library. Tomie De Paola's *The Clown of God* and Isaac Singer's *Elijah the Slave* are excellent children's stories that can be used by the storyteller.

Christ Legends by Selma Lagerlof is a book that contains a number of fine stories, some particularly suitable for Christmas.

Stories

The Woman in Wood
Although I have only heard this story in oral form, I am told that it finds its basis in an old Russian folktale. I first heard it from the late Ken Feit, a marvelous storyteller.

In an unknown forest, not far from anywhere, lived a carver, a tailor, and a teacher. They had dwelt together many years and were close friends.

The carver had a lifelong dream. Forced to carve bowls and

small figures to make a living, he longed for an opportunity to carve a life-size statue of a human being. One day he discovered a piece of wood that seemed to be just right for his project.

"Oh, do start carving," said the tailor.

"I can hardly wait to see the results," shouted his friend the teacher.

Encouraged by his two loyal companions, the carver began the task of whittling and cutting and slicing the wood. Like the master craftsman he was, he approached the project with great love and care. The days turned into months, and one day the carver announced, "My masterpiece is finished."

Finished it was. Before them stood the most beautiful statue of a woman they had ever seen. "Carver," they said, "this is your finest piece of work."

The tailor stood still for a few moments and then said, "I would like to offer something to the woman in wood. I would like to make a fine dress."

Soon the tailor was cutting and snipping, and before long he presented the woman in wood with a beautiful new dress. When it was draped over her, they all agreed that she was more lovely than ever.

Now the teacher stepped forward. "I too would like to offer the woman a gift. I would like to share with her all the great ideas that I have read or thought." Day after day he sat before her telling her of great thoughts.

Then one day a special magic took place. The woman in wood came alive. The three men were ecstatic and danced about singing and clapping. When the rejoicing was over, however, they began to argue over who owned the woman.

"She belongs to me," argued the carver. "If it were not for my dream and my carving skills, she would not be alive."

"She is mine," said the tailor. "It was I who gave her beauty."

"Before I taught her," the teacher reasoned, "she was only a woman in wood. It is her mind that made her human. She belongs to me."

It was no use; they simply could not settle the argument. In desperation they turned to a wise old man who lived further in the woods. Together the four of them traveled to his house.

After he listened carefully, the wise old man said, "Carver, you have done a magnificent job. I am certain that the woman is grateful for your love and your dream." Turning to the tailor, he said, "And tailor, I have never seen such a beautiful dress. It would add charm to anyone who wore it. I am certain she is grateful for your gift." Next he smiled at the teacher. "Teacher, you have given greatly of yourself. I am certain the woman wishes to thank you a great deal for sharing your fine secrets."

"But," he concluded, "the woman belongs to none of you. She belongs to herself. No one can own another person."

The woman in wood was overjoyed. "Thank you, wise old man!" she shouted. "Thank you for setting me free."

"I did not set you free," protested the wise old man. "You have always been free. You are free to choose anyone you want."

"Then I choose you!" the woman said enthusiastically.

The wise old man blushed before he spoke quietly. "I am honored that one as beautiful as you would choose me. I must tell you, however, that I choose not to be married. I prefer to live alone."

The woman was clearly disappointed. For a moment the tears trickled down her cheeks. After a few minutes she straightened and smiled. "Perhaps it is best if I do not marry just now," she said thoughtfully. "Perhaps I need to experience more." With that she kissed the carver, and the tailor, and the teacher, and the wise old man, thanking them individually. Then she simply left them all with a wave of her hand and went into the world.

For the Sake of the Animals

This is an old Jewish folktale that I have adapted. Behind this story lies the vision of the peaceable kingdom and the dream of shalom.

Alexander the Great once came upon a village hidden in a remote part of Africa. The people, he discovered, were peace-loving; they had never been involved in war. He was greeted warmly by all and brought as an honored guest to the hut of the chief.

As the two leaders sat in conversation, two citizens entered the hut asking that the chief serve as a judge over their dispute. "I bought a piece of land from this man," the first began. "While plowing, I discovered a treasure which he refused to take. When I bought the land for a meager price, I had no idea there would be anything of value buried on it."

The second man was quick to speak. "When I sold him the land, I gave up all rights to anything found on the property. The treasure clearly belongs to him."

The chief summarized the arguments until both men indicated that he clearly understood the case. After some reflection, he spoke to the first man. "You have a son, I believe?"

"Yes, sir."

"And you," he said to the second, "have a daughter?"

"Yes."

"Let your son marry your daughter," the chief concluded. "Give the two of them the treasure as a wedding gift." The two men looked at each other, nodded, and bowed to the chief before leaving.

Alexander expressed surprise over the verdict. "Was my judgment unjust?" the chief asked.

"Oh, no," Alexander said.

"What would you have done in your country?" the chief asked.

"In my country, either the men would have fought over the treasure to keep it for themselves or the government would have confiscated it."

The chief was shocked. "Does the rain fall in your land?"

"Yes."

"Does the sun shine?"

"Yes."

The chief thought for a moment. "Are there animals that graze on the green grass?"

"Certainly," Alexander replied. "Thousands of animals of different varieties."

"Ah," nodded the chief. "It must be for the sake of the animals that the Lord causes the rain to fall and the sun to shine, for certainly the people in your land are not worthy of his great blessings."

The Fisherman and His Wife

This ancient folktale, popularized by the Brothers Grimm, echoes the warnings of Jesus regarding humility in life. I often invite the listeners to join in on the chorus. They quickly learn the rhyme, and it seems to strengthen the telling.

There once was a fisherman who lived with his wife in a tidy but tiny cottage by the shore of a great lake. One day the man hooked a great fish, and, after a struggle, brought it on shore. Before he could open it with a knife, the fish spoke to him and told him that he was really an enchanted prince. Moved by his pleading, the man tossed the fish back into the sea and went home.

When he finished telling his wife about the adventure, she exploded. "Do you mean to tell me that you asked nothing of the prince in return for his freedom? You march back and tell the fish that you want a nice two-story home," the wife insisted.

Reluctantly the man returned to the shining waters and said:

> "Fish, O Fish out in the sea
> Come and hear my humble plea.
> Isabel my wedded wife
> Doesn't like our way of life."

Immediately the fish poked his head above the water and asked, "What does she want?"

"A two-story home," came the meek reply.

"Go back, she has her home," the fish answered.

Returning home, the fisherman was met by his wife in front of a simple two-story house with a small but charming flower garden in the front yard and lovely apple trees in the back.

"Now, wife," the fisherman said softly, "you will be satisfied."

The next day the wife announced that the house was simply too small, the yard and garden too tiny. "I want a castle," she announced. The man protested that this was all the house they needed, but when she insisted, he returned to the ocean where the water had turned yellow and green. Then he called out:

> "Fish, O Fish out in the sea
> Come and hear my humble plea.
> Isabel my wedded wife
> Doesn't like our way of life."

The fish appeared and asked, "What does she want?"

"Ah," said the fisherman, "she wants to live in a castle."

"Go home," the fish replied, "she is in her castle."

When the man returned, there was a great stone palace where the tiny cottage once stood, and Isabel was standing on the steps. They went inside where the great hall with a marble floor was filled with servants. In the dining room there was a mountain of food. Behind the house was grazing room for animals.

"This is what I call real living," said the woman.

"I hope you will be satisfied," the man muttered.

The next morning the wife announced that she wanted her husband to be king over all the land.

"I don't want to be king," he protested.

"Then I will be king," said Isabel. "Go back and tell the fish that I want to be king."

Slowly the fisherman returned to the sea, where the water had turned dark, and he cried:

> "Fish, O Fish out in the sea
> Come and hear my humble plea.

> Isabel my wedded wife
> Doesn't like our way of life."

"What does she want?" the fish asked.

"Ah—" said the man, "she wants to be king."

"Go back, she is king."

When he returned, the castle was even larger and more magnificent than before. There were soldiers in fancy uniforms marching all about and people who looked busy rushing in and out of the huge doors. In the middle of the great hall, Isabel sat on a throne of gold.

"Are you king, Isabel?"

"I am king."

"Are you satisfied?"

"No, I have decided to be emperor!"

"Oh, Isabel, not emperor."

"Yes, tell the fish I want to be emperor!"

"But, Isabel—"

"Go, I command you."

When he returned to the great sea, the water was murky, and it stank. The man looked out at the water and cried:

> "Fish, O Fish out in the sea
> Come and hear my humble plea.
> Isabel my wedded wife
> Doesn't like our way of life."

"What does she want?" the fish demanded.

"She wants to be emperor," the old man mumbled with head bent low.

"She is emperor."

When he returned home, the castle was larger and more noble than ever before. It fairly glistened with precious stones, and everywhere one could see barons and dukes. On the throne sat Isabel with a gigantic crown made of precious diamonds.

"You are emperor, wife?"

"Yes, I am emperor."

"How nice."

"Don't stand there, husband, I have decided to be pope!"

"No, Isabel, it isn't right. You can't—I won't—"

"As emperor, I command you to go!"

And he went, frightened and embarrassed. He went back to the sea that seemed to swirl and boil. As the winds howled, he shouted:

> "Fish, O Fish out in the sea
> Come and hear my humble plea.
> Isabel my wedded wife
> Doesn't like our way of life."

"What does she want now?"

"She wants to be pope."

"Go home, she is pope."

When he returned home, the fisherman could see that Isabel was pope. Surrounded by thousands of candles, she was dressed in magnificent robes sitting on the most splendid throne one could ever imagine. All around bishops and cardinals were deeply involved in conversation, and a gigantic cross stood towering over everything.

"You are pope, wife?"

"I am pope."

"You must be satisfied. There is nothing more."

"Wrong! I have decided to be God!"

"Isabel, have you gone crazy? You can be king, you can be emperor, you can even be pope, but you cannot be God."

The wife was insistent. "I want power not only over the people of the earth, but over the animals, and the forests, and even the heavens."

"Oh," the old man cried, "I beg you not to send me back to the fish."

"Go back this minute!" was her demand.

Outside a storm was raging and a wind was howling. It was nearly impossible to walk to the seashore, and as he opened his mouth to call the fish, great waves leaped over the stone wall and nearly drowned him. He cried:

> "Fish, O Fish out in the sea
> Come and hear my humble plea.
> Isabel my wedded wife
> Doesn't like our way of life."

"What does she want?"

"She wants to be God."

"Go home," the fish said briefly, "she is sitting in her cottage."

Immediately the winds ceased and the water became clear. When he reached home, the castle was gone, and in its place sat their simple cottage. And to this day the fisherman and his wife have lived in that cottage.

The Legend of St. Christopher

Christopher was a mild and gentle giant of a man who served the king of Canaan faithfully. Though he cared deeply for his lord, the king, he dreamed of serving the strongest master in the world. Taking leave of Canaan, he traveled until he came to the castle of the one who was said to be the greatest ruler in the world. When the king saw the size and strength of Christopher, he made him second in command and invited him to dwell in his court.

One day when a minstrel was entertaining the king, he sang a song about the devil. Whenever the name of the devil was mentioned, the king made the sign of the cross. Christopher asked the king about his actions.

"It is to ward off the devil," the king answered.

"Do you fear his power?" asked Christopher.

"Ah, yes," said the king, "he has great might."

Christopher shook his head sadly, "I must leave you, my lord, for I have a great desire to serve the most powerful one in this world. It seems the devil is that one."

Christopher began his search for the devil, wandering until he met a great company of knights. The leader of the knights, a man who appeared cruel and horrible, approached him and asked him what he wanted. "I am in search of the devil to be my master," said Christopher evenly.

"I am the one you seek," said the terrible knight. Christopher immediately bowed before the devil and promised his allegiance.

A bit later, as the company of knights walked together, they came upon a cross standing at an intersection. Immediately the devil turned to the side, taking his followers in a circuitous route until he finally came back to the highway.

"Why did we take this route?" asked Christopher.

At first the devil was reluctant to answer, but Christopher persisted. "There was once a man called Christ who was killed on a cross," the devil explained. "When I see his sign, I am afraid and attempt to avoid it."

"Then he is greater and more powerful than you," said Christopher. "I see that I have yet to find the one who is the greatest lord on the earth. I will leave you to find Christ, whoever he is."

Christopher began a long search for the one people called Jesus, the Christ. At last he came upon a pious hermit who welcomed him and began to teach him about Jesus. One day the hermit spoke to Christopher. "You are not ready to serve Christ. In order to do this you must fast."

Christopher said, "It is most difficult for me to fast. Ask me to do something else."

"You must wake early in the morning and pray long hours each day," the hermit said.

"Please," said Christopher, "find me a task more to my ability. I am not a man who can pray for long periods of time."

The hermit thought for a moment before he spoke again. "You are indeed tall and strong. You shall live by the river and carry across anyone who comes in need. In that way you will serve Jesus. I hope that our Lord Christ will one day show himself to you."

So Christopher began his life of service at the river, where the current was strong. There, with the help of a huge pole, he carried rich and poor alike over the treacherous river.

One day as he slept in his lodge by the river, Christopher heard the voice of a child calling, "Christopher, come carry me over." When he looked outside, he saw no one. Back in his lodge, he again heard the voice call. Again his search was unsuccessful. The third time he went outside, he found a child who begged Christopher to carry him over the river.

The giant took the child on his shoulders and began his walk across the river. As the water rushed against his body, the weight of the child was almost too much to bear. The further he walked, the more the water swelled, and the heavier the child rested on his shoulders. For the first time in his life, the giant Christopher was gripped with a fear of death. At last, using all his might, Christopher reached land and put the child down.

Lying nearly exhausted, Christopher spoke to the child. "I was in great trouble in the water. I felt as if I had the weight of the whole world on my shoulders."

Then the child spoke. "Indeed you have borne a great burden, Christopher. I am Jesus Christ, the king you serve in your work. This day you have carried not only the whole world, but the one who created the world. In order that you might know what I say is true, place your staff in the earth by the house, and tomorrow it will bear flowers and fruit." Then the child disappeared.

The next morning Christopher walked outside, and there he found his staff bearing flowers, leaves, and dates. Christopher now knew that he served the greatest and most powerful master in the world.

The Fowlers

I originally spotted this story in The Greek Passion *by Nikos Kazantzakis. The story's emphasis on discipline and its relationship to freedom makes it ideal for Ash Wednesday or the Lenten season.*

Two fowlers went up on a mountain to spread their nets. Carefully they set their trap before departing. When they returned, the nets were filled with doves. Desperately the birds flew back and forth trying to escape through the finely woven net.

Originally ecstatic over the large number of birds, the hunters, upon examining the birds more closely, were not very happy with their catch. "There will be no market for the likes of them," said the first. "No one will buy such skinny birds."

The second man shook his head. "A small investment in mash is all that is needed, and in a few short days we will have these birds nice and plump." Daily the two men brought feed and water, which the birds devoured quickly. Slowly they grew in size.

Only one dove refused to eat. As the others got fat, this obstinate bird got thinner, and it still struggled to get out of the net.

On the day the hunters came to take all of the birds to market, the dove who refused to eat had become so thin that, by a mighty struggle, it managed to squeeze through the net and fly away. It alone was free.

The Wind and the Sun
This is a fable attributed to Aesop.

The wind and the sun were involved in an argument, each claiming to be stronger than the other. Below them they saw a man wearing a heavy coat. "Let us see who can strip the man of his coat fastest," said the wind. The sun agreed and allowed the wind to begin. Gathering all of its strength, the wind came upon the man with a furious blast, causing the coat to flap about. But the harder the wind blew, the tighter the man held onto the coat.

When its turn came, the sun shone brightly upon the man, who quickly unbuttoned his coat. The warmer the rays cast by the sun grew, the more uncomfortable the man became, until he soon took the coat off and carried it on his arm.

Persuasion is better than force.

The Blind Men and the Elephant

Once there was a village where all the inhabitants were blind. When a man passed one day riding an elephant, a group of the village men cried out asking the rider to let them touch the great beast, for though they had heard about elephants, they had never been close to one.

About six of them were allowed to approach the animal, each being led to touch a different part of the body. After a time the rider left, and the blind men hurried back to their people to share the experience. "With what can you compare an elephant?" the people in the crowd asked their six friends.

"I know all about elephants," cried the man who had touched the animal's side. "He is long and narrow, built like a thick wall."

"Nonsense." shouted the man who had touched the elephant's tusk. "He is rather short, round, and smooth, but very sharp. I would compare an elephant to a spear."

A third, who had touched the ear, joined in. "It is nothing like a wall or a spear. An elephant is like a gigantic leaf, made of thick wool carpet. It moves when you touch it."

"I disagree," said the man who had handled the trunk. "An elephant is much like a large snake."

The fifth man shouted his disapproval. He had touched a leg of the great beast. "It is plain to me that none of you have described the animal accurately. It is round and reaches toward the heavens like a tree."

The sixth man, who had been placed on the elephant's back, cried out, "Can none of you accurately describe an elephant? He is like a gigantic moving mountain."

To this day the argument has not been resolved, and the people of that village have no idea what an elephant looks like.

The Stonecutter

This Japanese story, like the tale of "The Fisherman and His Wife," explores the nature of humility. In various versions the protagonist is named Nashti, Hafiz, and Huffi. Though I have used a name when telling the story, I refer to him in this written piece simply as the stonecutter.

There once was a stonecutter who lived alone. Though he had acquired great skill, he was very poor. He lived in a tiny bamboo hut, and his clothing was tattered.

One day as the stonecutter was working with hammer and chisel upon a huge stone, he heard the crowd gathering along the streets. By their shouts he could tell that the king was coming to visit his humble village. Joining in the procession, the stonecutter gazed in awe as the king, dressed in marvelous silk, was greeted by his subjects. "Oh, how I wish I had the power and glory of the king," he thought. "He has soldiers at his command. There is no one more powerful than our king."

His cry was heard in the heavens, and immediately the humble stonecutter was transformed into a powerful king. He found himself riding on a great horse, waving at the crowds of people who had flocked to see him. "This is power," he thought.

As the summer progressed, however, the new king watched the effects of the heat upon his people. Men and animals became weary, and plants withered under the powerful rays of the sun. As he looked at the sky, the new king realized that the sun was far more powerful than any earthly ruler. "How I wish I were as powerful as that," he thought. "I wish I were the sun." Immediately his wish was granted.

How the stonecutter relished his new role as the sun. He gloried in the power he felt as he surveyed the kingdoms below him. As he sent his bright rays to the earth, he watched kings and princes hide under their parasols, he watched as powerful warriors became weak under his gaze. Even the crops in the field were under his command.

Then one day a tiny cloud moved over the land, shielding the earth from the sun's bright rays. Seeing that here was something more powerful, he thought, "I want very much to be a cloud." Again, his wish was granted.

Now he blocked the sun's rays and felt important. He gathered all of his strength, becoming a gigantic cloud, and began to pour down rain on the earth. Rivers formed where previously there were none, and water flooded the streets of the cities and the farmland. Everything—trees, animals, people—seemed to be awed by his power. Everything except a huge rock that remained untouched. Again he had discovered something more powerful. "There is nothing," he thought, "as powerful as a rock. How I wish I were a huge stone." His wish was granted.

As a stone he remained motionless and powerful, unmoved by either sun or rain or anything that nature could bring. The stonecutter felt exempt from all of the forces that shaped the life and existence of those around him.

Then one day a man approached him, carrying a bag. When he stopped, he pulled out a chisel and a hammer and began to chip away at the rock. Realizing that the man with the tools was more powerful than any rock, he cried out, "Oh, I want to be a stonecutter."

Once again the heavens heard his cry, and he became a stonecutter. Once again he lived in a bamboo hut and made his living with hammer and chisel. And he was content.

Joshua and the Princess

There was once a man named Joshua who was the kindest and wisest man in all the land. He was equally comfortable talking with poor peasants or wealthy landowners.

So wise was he, and so broad was his knowledge, that the king often invited him to the palace for long conversations that ranged over many topics. He was such a frequent visitor that he was soon assigned a special room in the palace.

Joshua was a most contented man, but some felt he had a serious flaw. He was, in a word, quite ugly. It was only as one got to know Joshua, to sense his tender spirit, to hear the words flow out of his mouth like poetry, that one failed to notice how very plain he was.

The presence of Joshua in the palace pleased nearly everyone, with the exception of the king's youngest daughter. Accustomed to receiving favored attention from her father, she was not pleased to share his grace with the new stranger in their home.

One day, when he met her in the hallway, she spoke to him mockingly. "My father tells me that you are the wisest man in all the land, Joshua. Tell me, if you can, why does God choose to store such great knowledge in so plain a vessel?"

Joshua was silent a moment and then spoke quietly. "Can you answer a question for me, your highness? Does your father have any wine?"

"I thought everyone had heard of my father's great wine cellars," the young lady answered indignantly. "It is the finest wine in the land."

"Where does he store the wine?" the great man asked.

"Why, in large earthenware vessels," she answered quickly. She was no longer convinced that this man was as wise as his reputation.

"Earthenware!" Joshua roared with laughter until the young princess shouted at him in anger. "Forgive me," said Joshua, "but I am surprised that anyone of your father's stature would use such plain material. Even peasants store their wine in earthenware. I would expect that the *royal* wine would be kept in something more elegant, such as silver or gold." With that he bowed and left the young woman.

Quickly the princess marched to the wine cellars and told the chief steward to pour all of the wine out of the earthenware jugs into vessels of gold and silver.

Shortly after this episode, the king invited people to a great banquet where he served his best wine. As the guests sipped the good king's brew, their faces puckered up. The wine was sour.

When the king had tasted the wine, he called for the chief steward. "Who is responsible for ruining my best wine?" he demanded. The steward quickly explained what had happened. The king was furious and called his daughter to his table immediately.

After the banquet, the princess raced to Joshua's room and shouted, "Why did you trick me into pouring the wine from earthenware pots into vessels of silver and gold?"

"I am truly sorry that your father is angry, little one," began Joshua, "but perhaps you now see why God sometimes prefers to put wisdom in ugly containers. Wisdom, like wine, is best preserved in humble vessels."

Stories
of Great Lives

Keep on imitating me, my brothers. Pay attention to those who follow the right example that we have set for you.

Philippians 3:17

In our world the road to holiness necessarily runs through the world of action.

Dag Hammarskjöld

In a day when cynicism runs high and Saturday's heroes turn to grabbing for power, money, and headlines by Monday, we would do well to let our people know of the lives of the saints who have served God. Just as the lives of Washington and Lincoln help us understand a bit of what it means to be an American, so the lives of the faithful assist us in becoming disciples and imitators of Christ.

My first biographical storytelling, some 15 years ago, arose out of a failed attempt to share the great ideas of modern theologians with parishioners. The best of Barth, Bonhoeffer, and Niebuhr was greeted with the same enthusiasm most urban dwellers reserve for the livestock reports. How could Bonhoeffer's ethics be treated so shabbily?

Later I discovered that when I laced the ideas of Bonhoeffer around his life, new interest was aroused. Once those great theologians were seen as people, the same ideas, once ignored, were greeted warmly.

I should not have been surprised. My own admiration for the lives of Albert Schweitzer, Martin Luther King Jr., and St. Francis of Assisi preceded, even kindled, my interest in their thinking. I see now that the life stories of many great authors are equally important and infinitely more interesting than their written words. It is almost impossible to untangle the life events of Gandhi, King, or the Berrigans from their speeches and books.

Biography, though not as intimate as autobiography, still retains the effect of enfleshing the doctrines and tenets of our faith. Like sacraments, the lives of such people as St. Francis of Assisi or Teresa of Avila become visible words; their faith struggle is made available for our faith seeing.

As we paint our pictures of the faithful of God, we need to be aware of the temptation to cover their sins and ignore their failures. We can learn from the Scriptures that, rather than embarrass us, a knowledge of people's errors and limitations only makes them more accessible. We find it difficult to relate to persons who never cross the line of indiscretion or foolishness. Besides, as J. W. McClendon has reminded us, "Iconography is not biography."

On appropriate days, the lives of either ancient or more modern Christian saints can be woven into our homilies or treated separately. Events from the lives of John XXIII, Martin of Tours, or Martin Luther can help to illuminate the gospel. On appropriate occasions, the poetry of John Donne, introduced with a brief sketch of his life, can be a welcome change in our family gatherings. Even the music of Bach, Handel, or Ives gains greater appreciation if we know something of the life and faith of the people whose genius now graces our worship.

This kind of storytelling need not mean one more preparation for an already-busy minister. The task of telling a brief life story can be assigned to a lay person who has literary and oral speech skills. Given a few resources and some encouragement from the pastor, the right person can make a significant contribution to the life of the church by holding high the lives of the faithful.

Resources for Stories of Great Lives

In addition to biographies that are available on almost any of the great lives, a number of books with shortened histories are most useful tools for the teller of life stories. Butler's venerable *Lives of the Saints* comes in four volumes and is still the standard work in the field. I am particularly fond of *Inner Companions* by Colman McCarthy and *Saint Watching* by Phyllis McGinley, and *The Saint Book* by Mary Reed Newland also is a helpful work.

A number of novels and nonfiction works are well suited for adaption into shorter oral stories. Edna Hong's *Bright Valley of Love*, with its gripping story of Gunther, brings one face to face with the horrors of Nazi Germany and the courage and love of Christians who protected innocent life. *I Heard the Owl Call My Name* by Margaret Craven is the tender story of a young Episcopalian priest's mission to the Indians in a tiny village in Vancouver. Their gift to him is as great or greater than his to them; they teach him how to die.

Anyone familiar with the stories of Corrie ten Boom, particularly *The Hiding Place*, will recognize wonderful material for the adaptor's art. Vivid characters and a simple story line make this World War II thriller an excellent story to tell.

Those folks who wish to reflect on the relationship of biography and storytelling should see James William McClendon's *Biography as Theology*. The author explores the relationship between life stories and Christian theology and then tests his thesis with stories of Clarence Jordan, Dag Hammarskjold, Martin Luther King Jr., and Charles Ives.

Stories

Francis of Assisi

St. Francis is as close to a universal saint as we have. He is embraced equally by Catholics and Protestants. Even non-Christians find his life irresistible. Ecologists have discovered him of late after he has stood for years, a solitary figure, in backyard flower gardens. A simple man, we will find that it is not such a simple matter to summarize his creed or his appeal.

Born in the 12th century to a rich merchant of Assisi, a small city in Italy, he was named John. Later he took the name that was to stay with him—Francesco or "Frenchy." At 14 Francis was apprenticed to the family business, selling cloth. Though he was a diligent worker, he gained his reputation in social circles as a dashing young man rather than as a businessman.

When war broke out with Perugia, the 20-year-old Francis decided to be a hero. A tiny man, he purchased a full suit of armor in which to fight only to be the first captured in battle. As is true of so many great Christians, prison was a turning point in the life of the young soldier. When he was released, it seemed he had found a new sense of direction. Now his time, energy, and lavish spending was directed to the poor.

In a celebrated incident, shortly after his prison experience, Francis was riding his horse when he met a leper begging. Few normal people would feel any shame in admitting their fear of lepers, but Francis, after riding past the man, returned, dismounted, and kissed the man on the mouth before offering his coat.

One night while praying in St. Damian's Church, a tumble-down edifice, he heard the voice of God: "Francis, look at my house; it is in great disrepair; restore it for me." The building was in need, but the church at large was also crumbling. Soon Francis would be about the task of rebuilding both.

When Francis returned home from his prayers, he took a bolt of cloth, mounted his horse, and rode to market where he sold it. Soon word reached his father, whose patience was being sorely tested by his gadabout son. It was one thing to spend money on wild parties, but quite another to give it away to poor people. When Pietro Bernadone found his boy, he dragged him home through the streets of Assisi and put him in the cellar with irons locked to his legs. Only when the father left town on business was his mother able to release Francis.

Days later another confrontation brought father and son before the bishop, who acted as a judge. With a crowd looking on, the priest ordered Francis to return the money to his father. Francis obeyed by laying the money at his father's feet. Then he said, "The clothes are his as well. I give them back." He stripped himself and stood naked until the bishop gave him a robe. "No longer will I call him Father," declared Francis. "Now I will only say, 'My Father who art in heaven.'"

Sadly, the division was never healed. One can feel empathy for both father and son. One had been called to "Sell all you own and come follow me." It is not easy to be a father to one who answers such calls.

Later Francis spoke of that occasion before the bishop as his "wedding day." There he declared his fidelity to Lady Poverty, a bride to whom he remained faithful until death.

At first people jeered Francis as he appeared in rags through-out the town. It was not long, however, until the catcalls were silenced by the effective work of restoring St. Damian's Church. Soon a band of followers gathered around him, though he did not seek them. These "Franciscans" found their marching orders in the tale of the rich young ruler, the commandment to take nothing with you, and the words of Jesus, "Take up your cross and follow me." Called Friar Minors to designate their humility, they set forth to evangelize the world.

When the Friars entered a village, it was generally a signal for rejoicing. Work would cease, church bells would ring, children would wave branches and sing songs. Often people grabbed at the clothes of Francis, similar to the adulation shown contemporary rock stars. He would either speak in the churches or out in the open. Though his sermons were long, they were joyous. The theme was always the mighty love of God for all his world.

Love was a key to understanding Francis. He loved all the world—the sun, the moon, the fire, as well as insects and stones along the road. Francis believed that we cannot separate human life from the life of the air or land or water, a lesson we are only now relearning when all seem in short supply.

In his travels, the little friar would pick up worms along the path in order not to step on them. He would preach to flowers and trees and wrote canticles in honor of "Brother Sun" and "Sister Moon." Woodcutters on Franciscan property were enjoined to only trim trees, never to destroy them.

The power and influence of Francis soon spread throughout Italy. He settled disputes between the Bishop of Assisi and its mayor. He spoke before kings, royalty, and popes while clinging steadfastly to his vow of poverty. His spartan life, arising out of his vow never to own anything, would weaken the most vigorous of humans.

At one time Francis attempted to convert the Saracen sultan, Malekal Kamily. Though his mission was unsuccessful, the sultan was greatly impressed with the simplicity, sincerity, and wisdom of the tiny brother.

The rich and famous as well as the poor and humble sought him out, finding in this tiny saint a willing ear and a loving heart.

Late in life, when death was near, Francis paid dearly for a lifetime spent ignoring his body. As his sight failed, as he lay alone on a rough slab of wood, he cried out, welcoming sister death. In life and in death there was nothing that was a stranger to this one who found all of life centered in the love of Christ.

Teresa of Avila

Anyone who can combine discipline and celebration, prayer and dancing, and a sense of reform with a sense of humor is a person worthy of attention. Such a woman was Teresa of Avila, a 16th century mystic and a master of the one-liner.

When a serious visitor came upon Teresa in her convent devouring a bit of fowl at the banquet table, he complained that this ruined her ascetic image. "What will people think?" he asked her.

"Let them think what they want," she cried, with a drumstick in one hand. "There is a time for partridge and a time for penance." Amen.

Born to middle-class parents in the city of Avila, Spain, just 50 miles west of Madrid, Teresa came into this world about the time Martin Luther was brooding over the vices of the papists.

At age 20, against the severe opposition of her father, Teresa entered a Carmelite convent in her hometown. In those days, entering a convent was not much of a retreat from the outside world. Convent life reflected the permissive attitudes that pervaded the rest of society. Prayer was largely ignored, worship mattered little, and the life of the clergy was hopelessly secular. Young women who took vows continued to wear elegant jewelry, dined on delicacies, and entertained young men of the town in their sitting rooms.

Her early years in the convent were more marked with illness than the zeal we have come to associate with her. For nearly 30 years Teresa suffered from fits, tumors, and broken bones. Only when her vocation with God was finally in order, at age 45, did the physical ailments disappear.

Initially Teresa participated fully in convent life as she found it. When she discovered it was unable to satisfy her deep spiritual hunger, she began to dream of a reform movement based on a rigorous life of work and prayer. She longed for an order that offered an alternative to the affluence found in most contemporary orders.

Her initial efforts for reform met with vigorous opposition, not only from nuns and clergy, but the nobility and townspeople as well. Everyone, it seemed, had a stake in the casual form religion had taken. One cleric described Teresa as "a relentless gadabout who teaches as if she were a doctor of the church." Four centuries later, the church finally recognized her as such and granted her a position alongside Augustine, Thomas Aquinas, and other giants.

Teresa was not easily discouraged. When she met local resistance to her idea, she went directly to Rome and finally secured permission to begin her convent, a place called St. Joseph.

Beginning with three nuns, the small group lived in almost perpetual silence as well as austere poverty. Their habits were made of serge, and when they replaced ordinary shoes with sandals, they were nicknamed "The Barefoot Carmelites." The order fasted regularly.

Though the life of Teresa's order was rigorous, it was not dull or joyless. Music and dancing were a regular part of convent life. "Virtue and merriment go hand in hand," she exclaimed. "Just because the order is austere, there is no need for austere people," a distinction that contemporary culture has nearly lost.

Soon her order was flourishing, and she was asked to begin another. The need for discipline, for an alternative to the affluence of her time, was evident. In all she founded 32 convents and almost singlehandedly began a reform movement that swept Spain.

During her long hours of prayer, Teresa frequently was led to ecstasy and rapture. Her mystical experiences enlightened her nuns and attracted hundreds of pilgrims. Two of Teresa's books, *The Interior Castle* and *The Way of Perfection,* written as instruction manuals for her order, became contemplative classics.

Teresa became a tutor of other mystics, including St. John of the Cross, a diminutive monk who formed a monastery with another man. Teresa referred to the two of them as "a monk and a half."

Like so much of the rest of her life, Teresa held her mystical moments in perspective. Contemplation and action are never to be separated, she taught. Just as the active life is barren without contemplation, so the contemplative life is empty without action.

Nor did her great mystical moments mean that she lost her sense of humor. Even her reported conversations with God were filled with wit and charm. Was God beginning to sound a little bit like Teresa?

Once she confided to God that, "If I had my way, that woman wouldn't be the mother superior." God answered, "If I had my way, she wouldn't either."

Another time when Teresa was attempting to cross a stream, she slipped off her donkey and fell headlong into the water, nearly drowning. It is reported that God reminded Teresa that he chastises those he loves. "I treat all my friends this way." Teresa turned her eyes heavenward and sputtered, "No wonder you have so few friends, when you treat the ones you have so badly."

"Lord, save us from sullen saints," this grand woman once observed. Her petition is raised once again in our own generation, a time that reveals prophets who identify with the woes of the world but live without a sense of celebration. Likewise, we have thousands in this "me generation" who make pleasure and enjoyment the center of existence. In our time, like the day of Teresa, we need a reformer with a sense of humor. We need a person who can combine the rigors of discipline with a sense of joy. We need people who will remind us that there is a season and a time for everything, a time for feasting and a time for fasting, a time for penance and a time for partridge. We need a movement to restore a sense of holiness without losing a sense of mission. We need a Teresa.

Martin Luther

Every year on Reformation Sunday I tell the story of Martin Luther. The tradition began when I discovered that children assumed we were talking about the great civil rights leader whenever we mentioned the reformer's name.

Nearly 500 years ago, though there were many countries in what we now call Europe, there was only one church. There also was only one political ruler. This ruler was not only the head of the government, but he also was in charge of the church. He was called the pope.

The pope lived in Italy. Hundreds of miles to the north, in a country we now call Germany, there was a law student who was headed home when a great storm arose. Lightning filled the sky, and a fierce wind blew down branches that fell at his feet. In great fear the student cried out, "St. Anne, save me; I will become a monk."

He was saved, and true to his word, he became a monk. Living in a monastery, he spent his time performing simple tasks and attending worship five to seven times a day. His name was Martin Luther.

Though he was very bright and worked hard at his vocation, Martin was rather unsettled. He fasted up to three days a week, slept without blankets in freezing weather, and went to confession several times each day, all in an attempt to please God. Martin believed that God was very good and that we are very evil. It followed that God must be very angry at us for being so evil.

During his lifetime, the most popular religious picture displayed Christ the Judge sitting on a rainbow, a sword in one hand and a lily in the other. Below, evil people were being pulled by the hair into the flames of hell. No wonder Luther was so unsettled.

When nothing he did seemed to help, Luther turned to the saints. It was widely believed that the saints of God had been so good that they had accumulated a surplus, a treasury of goodness that was available for others. First Martin looked to the Virgin Mary and St. Anne for aid. They seemed to offer no assurance. Later he was to discover that no human being has any extra goodness to give anyone else. He discovered that God alone can grant us forgiveness. And, Luther discovered, God does. As he read the letters of Paul, he heard the words, "The just shall live by faith." Trust God, they seemed to say, and his love will come to you. We need not fret about pleasing God, he forgives us and loves us as we are.

When Luther made his "discovery," he was living in the province of Saxony, in the city of Wittenberg. One day a man by the name of Tetzel came to town to sell indulgences . . . but I am getting ahead of my story.

Albert of Brandenburg wanted to be a bishop. Actually he was a bishop of two areas, but he desired to be bishop of a third. The pope was willing to make Albert bishop if Albert would give him 12,000 ducats, that is, 12,000 gold pieces. "A thousand," said his holiness, "for each of the twelve disciples." Albert countered, "A more reasonable figure would be 7000, your grace, a thousand for each of the seven deadly sins." They compromised at 10,000, a thousand for each of the Ten Commandments.

Albert, however, didn't have 10,000 gold pieces. The solution the pope offered was to give Albert permission to sell indulgences, pieces of paper that said your sins were forgiven. Buy an indulgence and you were certain to go to heaven.

When Tetzel arrived at Wittenberg, where Luther was both a teacher and pastor of the Cathedral Church, the great drama began. Luther was irate. Privately he ranted, "You can't do things like this. Money can't buy the forgiveness of sins."

On the eve of All Saints' Day, Luther marched to the cathedral, and there on the great wooden door that served as a community bulletin board, he nailed 95 theses, that is, 95 arguments for debate. People quickly copied the theses down and ran them off on a new device called a printing press. Soon they spread all over Germany.

The initial reaction was predictable. Albert was angry, and the pope was furious.

Luther's purpose in posting the theses was to gain the opportunity to debate the indulgence issue. He soon got his wish, with the finest debater the church could produce, John Eck. During the discourse, Luther's opponent appealed to the authority of the pope. "I am right," Eck said, "because the pope says so."

Luther shouted back, "Then the pope is wrong. He is human, and he can make mistakes. Only the Word of God, only the Bible can be trusted in matters of faith."

Though the leaders of the church were clearly shocked at his remarks, Luther quickly became a hero all over Germany. Some admired him simply because they were proud of a German priest standing up to an Italian pope. Others were tired of German money going out of the country, while still others simply believed his calls for reform were greatly overdue.

In 1521, in the city of Worms, Luther was ordered by his church to take back what he had said and all that he had written or be banned from the church. He answered:

My conscience is captive to the Word of God. I will not take back anything, for to go against conscience is neither honest nor safe. Here I stand, I cannot do otherwise. God help me.

They expelled Luther from the church, making him a criminal. Anyone was free to kill him and in so doing become a hero. On his way home from the trial, he was captured by a group of hooded men on horseback. Most people later believed that he was killed. The men, however, were friendly. They had come to make certain Luther was safe. They took him to the Wartburg Castle to live until things became easier. While he lived at Wartburg, Martin translated the Bible into German for the first time.

Martin Luther had no desire to split the church, but it did split. He always hoped that the church would change, re-form. People thus called this period "The Reformation." Those who followed him, who protested against the errors of the church, were soon called Protest-ants or Protestants.

During the early years following Luther's excommunication, changes did take place. Worship changed from Latin to German, and a great emphasis on congregational singing developed using German folk tunes. The sacraments were reduced from seven to two, and people were allowed to have both bread and wine rather than just the bread.

Luther wrote hymns, teaching materials, and, in general, shaped the church for hundreds of years to come.

Several years ago, *Time* magazine, in a cover story on Martin Luther, declared that three men since the first century had changed the way the world thinks: Jesus, Karl Marx, and Martin Luther. However one counts, Luther is one of the great figures of history.

Today there are 80 million people in the world that call themselves "Lutherans" or "Evangelicals." More than eight million of those people live in the United States. All of this began a little over 460 years ago when a small town pastor had the courage to stand before princes, bishops, and popes and say, "The Bible is the sole authority for our faith and lives."

Martin of Tours

Born in 316 in lower Hungary, Martin was the son of a Roman soldier. Though his parents were not believers, in his early teens he came into contact with Christians who had a great influence on his life. In those days positions in the army were hereditary, offering Martin little choice but to begin a career in the service. This career would be brief and most unconventional.

At his commission, Martin was granted a servant whom he treated as an equal. Other soldiers were shocked to witness Martin polishing the boots of his servant or sharing his meal.

One day when a group of soldiers met a beggar at the gate of the city, each of them passed him by. When Martin reached the man, he leaped from his horse and cut his beautiful warm coat in two, offering one piece to the beggar and wrapping himself in the remaining piece. That night he dreamed that Christ spoke to others about him: "Martin, though still a catechumen, has clothed me with his garment." For Martin it was a sure sign that he was to become baptized. He did.

At his baptism, Martin, like a majority of the Christians of that time, became a pacifist. His immediate request to be released from his commission was denied. Later, when an opportunity arose for him to address Emperor Constantine II in person, he reiterated his request, saying that he desired to become a monk. The emperor declared that Martin would indeed go to battle, at the point of a sword if necessary. Bowing to the emperor's demand, Martin announced that he would go to battle, but he would not bear arms. That night, imprisoned, he prayed until sunrise. Before the battle began, the enemy surrendered. Martin was quickly given his release.

For a time he studied under St. Hilary in France. On a return trip to Italy, he was captured by robbers on his way across the Alps. When they asked him his name, he simply answered, "A Christian." When asked if he was afraid, he assured them that he had never felt more secure, but that he grieved for the condition of his captors. Legend tells us that before he left the robbers had been converted.

In Italy his main goal was to lead his parents to faith. His mother became a believer, but his father did not.

Martin returned to France where he took up residence in a monastic community. There he gained a reputation as a devout and humble man of faith. After 11 years he was elected, without his consent, to be bishop of Tours. Martin refused. Legends differ regarding his ultimate election. One says that as a ruse he was invited to attend to a sick woman in Tours. When he arrived, a crowd surrounded him and forced him to become bishop. Another tale is that when people came to find him and make him bishop, he hid, only to have his pet goose give away his hiding place.

Though the great majority of people in Tours favored his election as bishop, it was by no means unanimous. Many people objected to the monk on the grounds that his appearance was poor, his garments sordid, and his hair unkempt. Nevertheless, he was consecrated on the spot.

At first the new bishop lived in the church itself. Later, in 371, he moved out of this grand cathedral into a cave just outside the city. There he had more quiet and could avoid the trappings of the office, living in poverty. Quickly people moved nearby, forming a small but rigorous religious community.

Martin was a diligent worker, a man who regularly visited the homes of his people. When he found it too difficult to reach everyone, he organized the people by areas, or parishes, and assigned priests to each group. His organization is the standard for Catholic churches to this day.

Though Martin was deeply loyal to those who were a part of the worshiping community, his great love was to work with those who were outside the Christian faith. In fact, it was as an evangelist that he enjoyed his greatest success.

His greatest gift to the church was the manner in which he conducted the office of bishop. Two incidents stand out.

When Maximus became emperor through highly dubious means, Martin opposed him openly. In order to gain the bishop's favor, the new emperor held a banquet, assigning Martin a seat of honor. When it came time for a ceremonial drink, Maximus declined to drink first. Instead, he offered the cup to Martin, assuming that the bishop would be forced to return it to him, thus confirming his office. All eyes turned as the bishop finished his drink. Slowly he moved to the far end of the table and offered the chalice to a simple parish priest, declaring loudly that it was wrong to assume that there was any more noble office than that of a presbyter.

Later in his ministry, the church faced the teaching of a man by the name of Priscillianus who taught a form of gnosticism. Priscillianus said that the true essence of Christianity was through a secret knowledge that only an elect few could and would know. Martin joined a number of bishops in opposition to this teaching, but when a group of prelates arranged the death of the heretic and his followers, Martin was outraged! He immediately refused to commune with those who carried out the sentence, and for the next 16 years of his life he would not even attend meetings with the bishops involved. There was, he announced, a more excellent way to solve disagreements.

When he died at 80 years of age, thousands attended his funeral. He has been declared the patron saint of Norway and the patron saint of winemakers. (Any man who can manage to inspire those two groups is one who is worthy of attention.)

Martin of Tours, a simple bishop who discovered that the gospel and peacemaking are one. He knew that there are battles to be fought for truth and right, but the weapons need not be ones of violence. Blessed are the peacemakers, for they will be called children of God.

John XXIII

My father, who said he never felt comfortable without a knife in his pocket, used to explain his down-home ways by quoting the old saw, "You can take the boy off the farm, but you can't take the farm off the boy." How surprised he would have been to see that this old saying referred not just to displaced farmers, but even to popes.

John XXIII, the vicar of Christ, successor of St. Peter, bishop of Rome, and spiritual head of the world's Roman Catholics, can best be known and understood as a pope who never lost his farm-boy touch.

A man of wit as well as humility, John described his family background by saying, "There are three ways in Italy for a man to lose his money—women, gambling, and farming. My father chose the most boring of the three."

Born the eldest son of a peasant family that had farmed the same land in Lombardy, in northern Italy, for nearly 300 years, Angello Roncalli was shaped by the values, spirit, temperament, and faith of his simple family. Recognizing the value of his roots, Angello Roncalli returned to his home in Soto Il Monde for a month-long visit every year of his life until he was elected pope at age 78.

From birth it was assumed that Angello would be a priest. At age 14 he entered seminary, and, following ordination, he was assigned to Bergamo, a village just 13 miles from his home. There the unassuming but efficient Roncalli was appointed secretary to Bishop Giacomo Radini-Tedeschi, an active, social-minded man. From this bishop Fr. Angello caught a vision, not only for religious reform, but of the need for the church to identify with working people, a vision that would appear nearly a half-century later as church policy in his famous papal paper, "Pacem en Terris" (Peace on Earth).

Part of Roncalli's education came when he was drafted during World War I (Italy had no exemption for priests) to serve in the medical corps. There he learned firsthand of the horrors of war. As with most of his assignments, Roncalli served not as much with brilliance as with faithfulness.

In 1921 Pope Benedict XV appointed Roncalli to head the Sacred Congregation for the Propagation of the Faith, a mission that took him all over Europe. In each place he visited, he developed deep personal friendships that lasted through the time of his papacy.

In 1924 Roncalli received the first of a number of appointments to largely non-Catholic countries. In all he spent nearly 20 years of his life in Bulgaria, Turkey, and Greece. In each country he learned to appreciate local culture and customs, and he also learned the language in order to preach in the tongue of the people.

It was in Turkey and Greece that the future pope developed the ecumenical spirit that was to influence the Second Vatican Council nearly 40 years later. Though he could not and did not break through the official barriers that separated the Orthodox church from the Roman church, he visited Orthodox seminaries, developed friendships with church officials, and managed to thaw a bit of the chill from the official posture of the two bodies.

In Turkey, Roncalli cheerfully ordered secular clothes when

the anticlerical government banned religious garb from being worn outside church buildings. He introduced the Turkish language in the liturgy and had the gospel read in the vernacular. In short, his experience in Turkey and Greece played an important role in shaping the spirit of his papacy and the Roman Catholic Church as well.

This developing ecumenical spirit was not limited to other Christians. In 1944, alarmed with the news of the treatment of Jews by Germans, Roncalli met with a representative of the American War Refugee Board and proposed a simple plan to save Jewish lives. Baptismal certificates would be made available to any Jews who wanted them, no strings attached. In Budapest, in 1944, nearly all Catholic churches became refuges for Jews. When the Russians finally took over the city, nearly 100,000 Jews had been spared.

After the war, Roncalli was appointed papal nuncio to France. There he charmed the French with his wit and won them with his warmth. For eight years he walked the streets of Paris helping to heal a church that was deeply divided by the war.

Once, when entering a room together, the chief rabbi of Paris said, "After you, Excellency."

"No, no," Roncalli replied, "the Old Testament before the New."

Though the Vatican was alarmed with the Catholic Worker movement in France, Roncalli clearly was not. "Certainly they are a bit far out," he confided, "but without a touch of holy madness the church cannot grow."

In 1953 he was named cardinal and appointed patriarch of Venice, a post he expected to hold until his death. When Pope Pius XII died in 1958, as cardinal of Venice he went off to Rome to participate in the election of a new pope.

In the Holy City, the college of cardinals was deadlocked for 10 ballots. On the 11th, a compromise elected Cardinal Roncalli the 261st pope. It was an honor he neither sought nor wanted.

Most observers believed that Roncalli would be an interim pope. At 78 years of age, he was not expected to serve long or to change anything. The surprises, however, were quick in coming. First, he chose a name that had been unused for several centuries; he became John XXIII. In a quiet way, by his marvelous wit and humility, he began to put his mark on that dusty Roman office.

In an audience with the editor of the official Vatican newspaper, the first in 12 years, the new pope began by congratulating the editor on a job well done. Soon his concern surfaced. The paper was fond of saying "The Illuminated Holy Father" and "The Highest Pontiff." It frequently prefaced his remarks with such phrases as, "As we gather from his august lips." The new pope put it directly to the editor. "Let us have a style that suits the times. Wouldn't it be better to simply say, 'The pope says this, or the pope did that?' "

Once while visiting the Hospital of the Holy Spirit in Rome, a hospital administered by a religious order, the mother superior introduced herself saying, "Most Holy Father, I am superior of the Holy Spirit."

"Well," the pope replied with a twinkle in his eye, "I must say, you are lucky. I am only the vicar of Jesus Christ."

Unable to endure the silent dinners that were a papal custom, he soon invited people to join him for meals and implored them not to kneel when they came into the room.

During Lent, John XXIII revived a 1300-year-old papal custom and walked the stations of the cross along with the masses, who gleefully named him "Johnny Walker." He visited sick children in hospitals, made surprise visits to convents, and, on Christmas, visited the prisons of Rome. At heart the new pope was still a pastor.

Next John began the process of making the church a bit more catholic, and a bit less Roman. He created 55 new cardinals, including the first African and Japanese. He invited the archbishop of Canterbury to visit him, the first time the two great figures had met in 500 years.

Two papal letters marked his tenure as pope. The first, "Mater et Magistera," voiced the church's concern for the exploited poor in the colonial and emerging nations. In it, Pope John lamented the great disparity between the economically advantaged nations of Europe and North America and the underdeveloped lands in the rest of the world.

His greatest letter, however, was "Pacem in Terris," a letter addressed not just to Catholics, but to all people of good will. He pleaded for a movement away from the massive weapons of destruction. "Nothing is lost by peace; everything is lost by war," he wrote. Again, "If you want peace, work for justice."

John XXIII will be best remembered for calling the Second Vatican Council into session. Here he planted the seed for a new relationship with non-Catholics. Here the doors were thrown open for liturgical change—the singing of hymns and the celebration of the mass in the language of the people.

It was not John's proposals that shook the church as much as the simple act of "opening the windows and allowing the fresh winds to blow." By initiating a synod to discuss the state of the church and trusting the leaders to find adequate solutions, he brought the dawn of a new era to the Roman Catholic Church.

When he died in June of 1963, he had served as pope for only four years, seven months, and six days. Yet the Christian world had been touched by this elegant peasant. His dying words, spoken in Latin, were, "That they may be one."

At times the world is changed by great ideas or magnificent discoveries. John changed the world by his simple warmth and humility. These qualities were then, as now, what we need most desperately. They were then, as now, the purest gifts God can give.

John Muir

John Muir, founder of the Sierra Club, is perhaps America's best-known and best-loved conservationist. Few people are aware that Muir's great drive to save our nation's wild places arose out of his profound faith in God.

This story comes to us out of the Old West. It is the tale of a genuine western hero who was part warrior and part prophet. His battles were fought without guns, and his sermons were preached without a formal congregation. As we walk through unspoiled wildlands of the West, as we gaze at the raw beauty of our preserved forests, we celebrate the legacy of John Muir's courage and his religious convictions. It is largely because of his ministry, his crusade, that thousands of our nation's treasures still remain in their natural state.

Born in Scotland, Muir was the son of a strict Scotch Calvinist father who forced his children to read and memorize significant sections of the King James Bible. Though he later rebelled against his father's joyless brand of Christianity, John's attitude toward the created order was an outgrowth of his religious faith in a Creator who had wondrously made the world where humans, animals, and plants were interdependent.

In 1849, when John was 11, the family emigrated to America and settled in central Wisconsin, not far from Wisconsin Dells. Though the farm work was difficult, young John found time to read dozens of books as well as work on his inventions. His most famous early invention was an "early rising machine," a bed that put him on his feet at a desired time of the morning. The time he preferred was shortly after midnight. He would slip down the stairs and walk in the night, marveling at the wonders of God's creation.

At 18, Muir left home and enrolled in the University of Wisconsin, though he refused to participate in a degree program. Instead he took whatever classes caught his fancy. At first he focused on chemistry and geology, but as he wandered about the beautiful Madison lakes, his eyes were opened to the great beauty of the plants, "all alike, revealing glorious traces of the thoughts of God, and leading on and on into the infinite cosmos." His passion was now directed to botany. Between classes he took extensive foot tours through Wisconsin, Iowa, Illinois, Indiana, and even into Canada.

Though he preferred his studies of the natural order, he believed his real gifts lay in mechanics. He had invented clocks, machines, and a desk that arranged the books he was to study, allowing him 15 minutes before it pushed another book before him.

Leaving the University of Wisconsin, he took a job at a factory in Indiana where he invented machinery to increase the output of handles for brooms and rakes. His gifts were noticed, and he was offered a partnership in the business. One day he suffered an eye injury while working which ended his factory life. He bid farewell to mechanical work and began to devote the rest of his life to "the study of the inventions of God."

When the eye healed, he set out on foot from Indianapolis. His destination—the Gulf of Mexico. On the way he kept a daily journal of his observations of the flora, the forests, the geography, and his experiences with people. Edited after his death, these notes were published as "A Thousand Mile Walk to the Gulf."

When he finished his trek south, Muir headed west and settled in the Yosemite Valley, which became the center of his life for almost six years. He took long excursions into the mountains with a simple pack and a few loaves of bread, studying its plant life and its formation. He was the first to discover living glaciers in the Sierras, and he developed a theory that glaciers had formed the Yosemite Valley. Still in his early 30s and unknown in academic circles, his thesis was opposed by a distinguished geologist, Dr. Josiah Dwight Whitney, formerly of Harvard. Whitney maintained that glaciers had nothing to do with the formation of Yosemite. He argued that the floor of the valley had dropped down in some ancient cataclysm. Muir's rebuttal was simple: "The bottom never fell out of anything God made." Today no competent scientist doubts the significant role of the glaciers in the formation of Yosemite.

Though his contributions to science are significant, it is in the area of conservation that John Muir is remembered best. In a series of articles in two magazines, *Century* and *Scribner's Monthly,* Muir built a case for federal protection of western forest lands. "Any fool can destroy trees," he wrote. "They cannot run away; and if they could, they would still be destroyed, chased, and hunted down as long as fun or a dollar could be made out of their bark, hides, horns or backbones." Muir argued that just as government protects private orchards and shrubs, so mountain forests need safeguarding. His articles that spoke of sheep as "hooved locusts" alerted the nation to the danger to forests from private and commercial interests. "It took three thousand years to make these great trees," John wrote, "and since the time of Christ, God has cared for these trees, saved them from drought, disease, avalanches, and a thousand straining, leveling tempests and floods; but he cannot save them from fools —only Uncle Sam can do that."

And Uncle Sam did. Awakened by Muir's articles, Congress passed an act in 1890 empowering the president to create forest reserves. John was invited by a special commission to tour land that would eventually become national forests. In 1890, Yosemite was made a national park. In 1897, two Muir articles, written with the frenzy of a Hebrew prophet, alarmed the country again, causing more land to be saved from those who would cut everything that grew.

Muir's rhetoric was just as sharp in speeches as it was in ink. When asked by a wealthy woman whether California redwoods would make beautiful furniture, Muir replied, "Madam, would you kill your own children?"

In 1903, during his first term as president, Teddy Roosevelt slipped away for a three-day camping trip in the Sierras. His guide was John Muir. During the trip, the president saw Yosemite through the eyes of its foremost advocate. He listened to Muir's impassioned pleas for the protection of our forests and our need for additional parks while sitting with Muir around the evening campfire. During the next six years, Roosevelt set aside 148,000,000 acres of additional forest reserves and doubled the number of national parks.

In 1880, at age 42, Muir married for the first time. He and his wife, Louie, raised two daughters, and John left the wilderness long enough to throw his considerable efforts into managing fruit farms that his father-in-law had developed. Though he made a considerable sum of money, Muir was unimpressed with his new wealth. He gave away large amounts and continued to dress in wilderness fashion. His attitude toward money was best summed up in his comment about the very wealthy father of Averell Harriman. "Mr. Harriman is not nearly as rich as I am. He does not have all the money he wants, and I do."

Late in life, John Muir traveled throughout the world to study the grandeur wrought by the hand of God. He died in 1914 after losing a battle to preserve one last section of the Yosemite Valley.

A reluctant writer whose first book was published at age 56, John Muir helped awaken Americans to the need for the preservation of their country's beauty. He wrote as one captured by the awe and wonder of God's creation. "No synonym for God is so perfect as beauty," he wrote. "Whether as seen carving the lines of the mountains with glaciers, or gathering matter into stars, or planning the movements of water, or gardening—still all is beauty."

Thanks to John Muir, a significant portion of that unspeakable beauty has been preserved for all of us.

8

Modern Stories and Parables

Though my preference in stories, as in cheese, is for that which has a bit of age, I find that there are a host of excellent modern stories available for the storyteller. Found in a variety of sources, they await the process of becoming a part of the community's treasure. In this post-Gutenberg age, I expect the method by which stories become "folk art" will be quite different from that of an earlier time.

Folktales were passed down through the ages orally, each storyteller leaving the tale a bit different than he or she found it. In this sense, folktales have been shaped by the hopes, dreams, faith, and fears of generations of people. This constant revision gave each story its sturdy and enduring character. It has also made them stories of the people, by the people, and for the people.

Modern stories have not yet passed through the community. For the most part, they still bear the mark of a single author and consequently are found not in folk or oral form, but in a more polished or literary style—one demanded by the laws of publication.

Will these stories enter into the life of the community and be shaped by the events and moods of our time? Will these stories, like other folktales, lose their identities with single authors and take on the character of people-stories? If so, the method for developing folktales will have been reversed from earlier times, with the written stage now preceding the oral stage.

What follows, both in the resource section and the story section, are stories written by single authors. They are all modern insofar as they were written within the last 100 years or so. The Tolstoy selection may appear a bit old to be located here, but considering the age of folktales and biblical stories, 130 years is certainly in the modern era.

Resources for Modern Stories and Parables

I have carried a paperback edition of *The Great Short Stories of Leo Tolstoy* with me for almost 20 years. I have told "Where Love Is, God Is," "God Sees the Truth But Waits," and "A Spark Neglected Burns the House" at camps, women's meetings, and during church services. The reason Tolstoy is so attractive to me is that he writes with an oral voice, the way people speak. Thus his stories, primarily biblically based, lend themselves well to storytelling. The classic I have adapted and included later in this chapter, "Land Enough for a Man," is my favorite Tolstoy story.

Nathaniel Hawthorne is another writer whose short stories are close to the oral folk tradition. His tale "The Great Stone Face," the story of a young man who is shaped by his dream of justice, is particularly adaptable to the church setting.

James Carroll's "The Tinker King" is the story of a king turned tinker who "sees connections, is gentle with life and with death, and who knows that whenever anything dies a lot, he dies a little." It is found in Carroll's book *A Terrible Beauty.*

Oscar Wilde has written a couple of short stories that I have enjoyed telling. "The Selfish Giant," by discovering the need for self-giving, is brought face to face with a child who bears the marks of nails in his palms. The same self-giving theme characterizes "The Happy Prince." The prince is a statue in a park who gives up his beauty—rubies, sapphires, and gold—to the poor of the city. God alone, and a swallow, know of his gift.

The story of two caterpillars who forgo the drive to climb the "Caterpillar Pillar" and allow the power of death and rebirth to get them to high places has captured a wide Christian audience. *Hope for the Flowers,* Trina Paulus's book that includes this story, is about resurrection or, as she calls it, "the real revolution."

One of the best modern Christian writers is Flannery O'Connor. Though I am fascinated by her stories, I have yet to adapt any for telling. Two of her stories that seem well worth the effort are "The Artificial Nigger" and "A Good Man Is Hard to Find."

Stories

The "Nosy" Neighbor

This largely autobiographical short story was written after my family moved from an intimate village of 250 to the rather sterile privacy of a Detroit suburb. There we discovered that what was being nosy to some was a matter of caring to others.

Once there was a nosy woman—or at least her neighbors thought her to be so. When a door would slam at the house across the street, she would go to her window and peer through to see who had come home. When children would ride their bikes past her house making sounds like racing motorcycles, she would step outside and watch them. While working in her yard, she would frequently pause and look around to see what was happening at the homes in the neighborhood.

One of the neighbors—Mrs. A—said, "If someone sneezes three houses away, she'll shout *'Gesundheit.'* "

Mrs. B—another neighbor—said, "She knows what you bought at the store before you get it in the house."

Mrs. A always pulled her shades so the nosy neighbor couldn't see in. Mrs. B had her husband build a privacy fence to prevent the nosy neighbor from "spying."

One bright Sunday afternoon, two small boys, both three years old, were playing boats at Mrs. C's above-ground pool. They would place blocks of wood in the water and then splash, making waves in order that the "boats" would drift to the other side. They would then run to the other side and repeat the fun.

"Donald," the nosy neighbor said to her husband, "I just don't feel right about those boys playing at that pool."

"Unhuh," Donald muttered, puttering with his lawn mower.

A few minutes later the woman broke the silence again. "Those boys are leaning over the side of the pool."

"I'm sure their parents know what is going on, dear," Donald said, tightening a nut.

At the home of Mrs. A, the shades were drawn while the family watched TV. Behind the privacy screen, the B family was enjoying an afternoon cocktail party with some friends.

"Donald," there was an urgency in her voice. "I can only see one boy, and there is splashing in the pool. Donald, run over and see."

Without looking up, Donald agreed. "In a minute, dear." *"No! Now!"*

Donald rose obediently and trotted to the back fence which he leaped gracefully. He jumped across a drainage ditch that separated the two homes and ran up the hill to the pool. When he reached the edge of the pool, fear seized him. Face down, a small body lay still on top of the water.

Quickly he leaped into the water, grabbing the boy, and in one effort he scrambled out again. Now he was on the ground, pushing on the boy's back and awkwardly remembering words from long ago: "Out goes the bad air, in comes the good air." As he pushed he shouted loud—soon blurs that were people began to appear—sounds began to scramble together so that later he could not remember their sequence. Cries—sobs—squealing tires—sirens! Soon strong hands flipped the boy over and tense lips began to breathe into his mouth. As the ambulance sped away, he remembered the words, "He's breathing, he's going to be OK."

In all, just a few minutes had passed. Trembling, Donald and his wife embraced and then looked tenderly at their own children, seeing each of them as if for the first time.

Next door, the shades were still pulled at the home of Mrs. A. while loud laughter broke the silence behind the well-designed wooden fence of Mrs. B.

The Good Child Award

Sara was an active, likable child of seven—full of wonder and questions. Sara was always busy. Sara's teacher, who liked Sara very much, said to her, "Sara, sit down. Sara, don't talk. Sara, do your work."

When Sara came home she would tell her mother many things about school. She would tell her of the things she learned, of the songs they sang, of the things people said. She would tell her parents stories of her friends. She would say, "Today Mary got the Good Child Award," or, "Todd got the Good Child Award."

Her father asked, "Did you ever get the Good Child Award?"

"No," said Sara. "I guess I talk and walk around too much for the Good Child Award."

One day Sara came home excited. "Guess what? I got the Good Child Award!"

"Wonderful!" exclaimed her mother, who liked to know that her children were good. "Do you know why you received it?"

Sara laughed. "Today I was very sleepy in school. I laid my

head down on my desk, and I didn't say a single word all afternoon. Before I left school, the teacher said what a change had come over me and gave me the Good Child Award."

Land Enough

This story is adapted from Leo Tolstoy's "Land Enough for a Man."

There once was a man who had a small farm of 30 acres where he grew vegetables for his wife to sell at their roadside stand. The man worked by day at a factory in town and managed to farm the land early in the morning and on weekends. At night, when they would sit alone at the kitchen table, his wife would say, "Martin, we are most fortunate that our vegetables grow so well. People buy everything we grow."

But Martin was not satisfied and would say, "I do not have enough land. If I had more land, I could quit my job in town and farm full time."

Soon an opportunity arose, and Martin borrowed money to purchase a field of equal size adjoining his property. Since he kept his job in town to help pay for the field, he now worked far into the night preparing the land, planting and caring for the plants that grew lavishly and beautifully. When he would return late at night, his wife would say, "Martin, God has been good to us. The warm sun and the abundant rainfall have filled our stand, and still the people buy all we grow."

But Martin was not satisfied and would say, "I do not have enough land. If I had another farm, we could sell vegetables to the stores in town as well as at our stand."

Soon an opportunity arose, and Martin was able to purchase 140 acres nearby. He no longer worked in town. Although his wife worked faithfully by his side, there did not seem to be enough hours in the day. Early each morning he drove his produce truck to three small grocery stores who were eager to purchase his vegetables. When they had time together to talk, his wife would say, "Who could be more fortunate than we,

Martin? Our fields are full and we sell everything we grow."

But Martin was not satisfied and would say, "I do not have enough land. If I could buy more land, we could sell to the chain stores—that is where the real money is."

Soon an opportunity arose, and Martin purchased a farm of nearly 250 tillable acres. He closed the roadside stand, hired men to manage each farm, and a woman to truck the produce during the harvest season. He built refrigerated storage buildings so that he could sell when the prices were highest. Martin's wife did the bookwork while he supervised his many employees, including the seasonal help who migrated in to assist at harvesttime. He now sold to many small stores within a 40-mile area as well as to a national chain.

On weekends, when they would go out for dinner, his wife would say, "God is good to us, Martin. There is nothing we lack."

But Martin was not satisfied and would say, "I do not have enough land. If I could buy land south of here, we could grow other crops that our climate will not allow."

Soon an opportunity arose to purchase a large farm 300 miles south. Now Martin commuted between farms and began to work long hours on weekends.

After a very long day, Martin suffered a heart attack and died. He was buried in a small cemetery plot, seven feet long, four feet wide, and six feet deep. Just enough land.

The Butterfly

One good story reminds people of another. Once, when I finished telling a butterfly tale from the book Zorba the Greek, *a listener came to me and told of an event from her schoolteaching days. This is her story, as I remember it.*

While teaching school, a young woman purchased three cocoons for her class to observe. All of the children eagerly watched their development each day. One never did open, but the other two showed signs of life. Finally, one day, one of the cocoons broke open and a tiny head began to break through. Ronney, a boy who had followed the developments more closely than the others, watched with wide-eyed amazement as the butterfly struggled desperately to escape. Wanting to help, Ronney took a pencil and broke some of the material around the opening. When the butterfly emerged, it was crippled. Soon it died.

Ronney soon realized what had happened and cried to his teacher, "I only meant to help. It looked like it was in so much pain!"

The other butterfly struggled alone and emerged whole and beautiful. The teacher took the butterfly outside and allowed it to go free. Then she and the children skipped across the schoolyard waving and laughing as the butterfly tried its new wings.

When they returned to the classroom, Ronney was crying again. "I only meant to help," he sobbed.

Silence

Excerpted from The Town Beyond the Wall *by Elie Wiesel,* "Silence" *(my title) is a powerful story of the atrocities of hatred and war. Wiesel, himself a prisoner of the Nazis, relives the horror of that time through his novels. His style is as close to the oral form of storytelling as any living author.*

"The hero of my story," Michael began, "is neither fear nor hatred; it is silence. The silence of a five-year-old Jew. His name was Mendele. In his eyes the whole sweep of his people's sufferings could be read. He lived in Szerencseváros, which means in Hungarian the city of luck. One day the Germans decided to rid the country of what they called the Jewish plague. Feige, Mendele's mother, a beautiful and pious young widow, had a visit then from an old friend of her husband, a peasant who owned an isolated farm on the other side of the mountain.

" 'Take your son, Feige, and come with me,' the peasant said to her. 'I owe it to my friend to save his family. Hurry up, now!'

"It was night. The streets were deserted. The peasant led the widow and her son to where he had left his wagon. He had them get up into it, and then he said to them: 'I'm going to load the wagon. You'll be buried under a mountain of hay. It has to be done. I'll work two openings so you can breathe. But be careful! In heaven's name, be careful! Don't move! Whatever happens, don't budge! And most of all when we leave town, at the sentry station! Tell that to your son, Feige.'

"The widow took her son's face in her hands and as she stroked his hair very gently, she said to him, 'Did you hear? We must be silent. Whatever happens! It's our only chance. Our lives depend on it. Even if you're afraid, even if you hurt, don't call out, and don't cry. You can scream later, you can cry later. Do you understand, son?'

" 'Yes, Mother. I understand. Don't worry. I won't cry. I promise.'

"At the sentry station two Hungarian gendarmes, black feathers in their hats, asked the peasant where he was going.

" 'I'm going home,' he answered. 'I have two farms, two fields; the town lies between them. To move hay or wheat from one to the other I've got to cross the city. I've done it so often that the horses know the way all by themselves.'

" 'What are you hiding underneath?'

" 'Nothing, officers. Nothing at all. I swear it. I have nothing to hide.'

"The gendarmes drew their long swords from their black scabbards and drove them into the hay from all angles. It went on forever. Finally the peasant couldn't stand it any longer; he let out a whimper, and tried to smother it with the back of his hand. Too late. One of the gendarmes had noticed. The peasant had to unload the hay; and the gendarmes, triumphant, saw the widow and her son.

" 'Mama,' Mendele wept, 'it wasn't me who called out! It wasn't me!'

"The gendarmes ordered him off the wagon, but he couldn't move. His body was run through. 'Mama,' he said again, while bloody tears ran into his mouth, 'it wasn't me. I wasn't me.' The widow, a crown of hay about her head, did not answer. Dead. She too had kept silence."

An Invitation to Storytelling

The place was a suburb of Detroit in the early '70s. The speaker, Elie Wiesel. The subject, "After Auschwitz, Can We Still Believe?" Jews and Gentiles alike filled the great synagogue to listen to the recollections of one who survived the furnaces of Dachau. Thin and fragile, Wiesel stood at the podium for nearly an hour telling one story after another of the horror and despair of those bleak days in the '30s. His stories were of people confused with their imprisonment and sometimes destroyed with their release. Painfully, silently, the audience relived the events of Wiesel's young life when he was the only surviving member of his family.

Finally the stories ceased. His eyes dropped to the floor. There was no sound at all in that mammoth room for what seemed an agonizing eternity. Then he repeated the question, "After Auschwitz, can we still believe?" He shook his head slowly, sadly, "No, no, . . ." before concluding powerfully, "but we must!"

To those who uneasily filed out of the room that night, Buchenwald and Dachau once again became a part of their vocabulary. Through the eyes of the storyteller, they saw, even remembered, that in a small way Auschwitz had happened to them all. They remembered, both those who wore the star of David and those who bore the cross of Christ, that they were all Jews.

In the first century, a man by the name of Stephen was brought before the Sanhedrin. "He talks against the sacred temple and the law of Moses by saying that Jesus will tear down the temple and change our religious customs," they charged. In his defense, Stephen began by retelling the story of Israel and its unfaithfulness to God. He told stories that reminded those who listened that their people had always ignored their prophets. They had a history of being "stiff-necked." As Stephen spoke, the people remembered, and they stoned him for his efforts.

We are a forgetful people. Unless reminded, we are apt to forget our sordid history. We appear almost eager to ignore the dark moments of our past, our Vietnams and Nagasakis. The tragedy of forgetfulness, of course, is that we may be forced to relive those events again.

Storytellers help us remember. Through the recitation of Israel's history, the prophets reminded the people of their nation's harlotry. Alex Haley retold the story of the capture and transportation of black men and women to this country. He would not allow our nation to forget its sin against its black citizens. In *Bury My Heart at Wounded Knee,* Dee Brown has chronicled the often tragedy-stricken history of native Americans. All of these storytellers carry out their task, Henri Nouwen has reminded us, not to plague our memories, but to help us remember and, in remembering, confess in order that ultimately we will be made whole. Storytelling can be therapeutic.

However, it is not just the dark moments we tend to forget. We also fail to remember the good news. We forget the story of grace.

When the candle of hope burned dim in the Roman catacombs, Christians felt abandoned. "Where is God?" they asked. "Is this where faithfulness leads?" In those dark times, the storytellers stepped forward to recount the history of a God who suffered with and for his people. Through the stories that now comprise the gospel of Mark, they remembered the life of Jesus and how a hostile world turned against love's best hope, hanging him on a cross. In remembering, faith held firm.

When the days were long in Babylon, the Jewish people gathered to listen to the stories of the rebellion of their fathers and mothers and the steadfast love of God. The elders told stories of Yahweh rescuing them from the iron grip of Pharaoh and loving them into a nation. They told stories of how people turned their backs on God, and how God remained faithful. As these stories were told, their hearts were lifted.

We are a forgetful people. We need storytellers. We need someone to lay the drama of God's love before us. We need to be reminded of the uncommon grace of God. We need to hear the stories of the almost-too-good-to-be-true promises of God, the story of good news in the midst of the world's bad news.

This is an invitation to a new generation of storytellers to memorize and tell the stories of God. Though some of those stories will shock us and others will weigh heavy on our hearts, basically the storyteller's task will be a joyous one.

The main assignment will be to focus on the good news—the promise and the happily-ever-after of God's story.

Our invitation may seem strange to some who associate storytelling only with libraries and bedtime. Others will think that our stories are mere idle tales. We know them to be the foundation of faith and the essence of life. And that, as they say, reminds me of a story.

An old pastor visiting a county jail came upon a despondent young man. "Leave me alone, pastor. I'm no good," the young man moaned. "Everything I have touched has been bruised. I have influenced others to turn to a life of crime. I have deeply wounded the only ones who care for me—my mother, my wife, and our young daughter. There is no hope for me."

The old man was silent for a moment before he spoke. "The hurt that you have inflicted on others may never be healed. What you have done is most serious. What you need now is to find a new compass, a new way to walk." He paused before he continued. "We must begin by teaching you some new stories."

"Stories!" the young man thundered. "I speak to you out of despair and you talk to me of idle tales? I live without hope and you speak to me of happy endings? If my life is to be spent behind bars, I may need new facts, but I certainly do not need fiction."

When the outburst had subsided, the pastor placed a caring hand on the young man's arm. "Humor an old man. Listen to one tale."

Once a very bad man died and went before the judgment throne. Before him stood Abraham, David, Peter, and Luke. A chilly silence hung heavy in the room as an unseen voice began to read the details of the man's life. There was nothing good that was recorded. When the voice concluded, Abraham spoke.

119

"Men like you cannot enter the heavenly kingdom. You must leave."

"Father Abraham," the man cried, "I do not defend myself. I have no choice but to ask for mercy. Certainly you understand. Though you lied to save your own life, saying your wife was your sister, by the grace and mercy of God you became a blessing to all nations."

David interrupted, "Abraham has spoken correctly. You have committed evil and heinous crimes. You do not belong in the kingdom of light."

The man faced the great king and cried, "Son of Jesse, it is true. I am a wicked man. Yet I dare ask you for forgiveness. You slept with Uriah's wife and later, to cover your sin, arranged his death. I ask only forgiveness as you have known it."

Peter was next to speak. "Unlike David, you have shown no love to God. By your acid tongue and your vile temper you have wounded the Son of God."

"I should be silent," the man muttered. "The only way I have used the blessed name of Jesus is in anger. Still, Simon, son of Jonah, I plead for grace. Though you walked by his side and listened to words from his own lips, you slept when he needed you in the garden, and you denied him three times in his night of greatest need."

Then Luke the Evangelist spoke. "You must leave. You have not been found worthy of the kingdom of God.

The man's head bowed sadly for a moment before a spark lit his face. "My life has been recorded correctly," the man began slowly. "I am guilty as charged. Yet I know there is a place for me in this blessed kingdom. Abraham, David, and Peter will plead my cause because they know of the weakness of man and the mercy of God. You, blessed physician, will open the gates to me because you have written of God's great love for the likes of me. Do you not recognize me? I am the lost sheep that the

Good Shepherd carried home; I am your younger, prodigal brother."

And the gates opened, and Luke embraced the sinner.

"You see," the old pastor concluded, "I want you to learn stories, not as an exercise in fiction, but in order to walk in mercy. Stories will help you find your way."

Bibliography

Aesop's Fables. Based on a translation by George Fyler Townsend. Garden City: Doubleday, 1968 (out of print; other editions available).

Andersen, Hans Christian. *Andersen's Fairy Tales.* New York: Grosset and Dunlap, 1945 (out of print; other editions available).

Ausubel, Nathan, ed. *A Treasury of Jewish Folklore: Stories, Traditions, Legends, Humor, Wisdom and Folk Songs of the Jewish People.* New York: Crown, 1948.

Bainton, Roland. *Here I Stand: A Life of Martin Luther.* New York: Abingdon-Cokesbury, 1950.

Buber, Martin. *Tales of the Hasidim.* 2 vols.: *The Early Masters; The Later Masters.* New York: Schocken, 1947.

Buechner, Frederick. *Telling the Truth: The Gospel as Tragedy, Comedy and Fairy Tale.* New York: Harper and Row, 1977.

Butler, A. *Lives of the Saints.* 4 vols. Edited by Donald Attwater and Herbert Thurston. Westminster, Md.: Christian Classics, 1976.

Carroll, James. *A Terrible Beauty: Conversions in Prayers, Politics and Imagination.* New York: Paulist Press, 1973.

De Paola, Tomie. *The Clown of God.* New York: Harcourt Brace Jovanovich, 1978.

Harrell, John and Mary. *A Storyteller's Treasury.* Berkeley: Self-published, 1977.
————. *To Tell of Gideon.* Berkeley: Self-published, 1975.
Hawthorne, Nathaniel. *The Great Stone Face and Other Tales of the White Mountains.* Boston: Houghton Mifflin, n.d.
Henry, O. *O. Henry's New York.* Greenwich: Fawcett, 1962 (out of print).
Hong, Edna. *Bright Valley of Love.* Minneapolis: Augsburg, 1976.

Kazantzakis, Nikos. *The Greek Passion.* New York: Simon and Schuster, 1959.
————. *Zorba the Greek.* New York: Simon and Schuster, 1953.

Lagerlof, Selma. *Christ Legends.* Spring Valley, N.Y.: Floris Books (St. George Book Service), 1977.

McCarthy, Colman. *Inner Companions.* Washington, D.C.: Acropolis, 1978.
McClendon, James William Jr. *Biography As Theology: How Life Stories Can Remake Today's Theology.* Nashville: Abingdon, 1974.
McGinley, Phyllis. *Saint Watching.* New York: Viking, 1969 (out of print).

Morrison, Alison and Trevor. *Aesop and the Bible*. London: A. R. Mowbray, 1963.

Newland, Mary Reed. *The Saint Book*. New York: Seabury, 1979.

O'Connor, Flannery. "A Good Man Is Hard to Find." In *Three by Flannery O'Connor*. New York: New American Library, 1980.

Paulus, Trina. *Hope for the Flowers*. New York: Paulist, 1972.

Rice, Charles. "The Preacher As Storyteller." *Union Seminary Review* 31:3 (Spring 1976), p. 182ff.

Sawyer, Ruth. *The Way of the Storyteller*. Rev. ed. New York: Penguin, 1977.

Singer, Isaac. *Elijah the Slave*. New York: Farrar, Straus and Giroux, 1970.

Ten Boom, Corrie and John and Elizabeth Sherrill. *The Hiding Place*. Old Tappan, N.J.: Revell, 1971.

TeSelle, Sallie. *Speaking in Parables*. Philadelphia: Fortress, 1975 (out of print).

Tolkien, J. R. R. *Tree and Leaf*. Boston: Houghton Mifflin, 1965.

Tolstoy, Leo. *The Short Stories of Leo Tolstoy*. New York: Bantam, 1960 (out of print).

Wagenknecht, Edward, ed. *Stories of Christ and Christmas*. New York: McKay, 1963 (out of print).

Wiesel, Elie. *Messengers of God: Biblical Portraits and Legends.* New York: Random House, 1976.

———. *Souls on Fire: Portraits and Legends of Hasidic Masters.* New York: Random House, 1972 (out of print).

———. *The Town Beyond the Wall.* New York: Holt, Rinehart and Winston, 1967.

Wilde, Oscar. *The Happy Prince and Other Stories.* New York: Penguin, 1962.